''The literature of spiritual progress...' is the motive that lies behind the new work of Dom Hubert van Zeller. Written in his usual hard-hitting style, it does not always make comfortable reading in the sense that it has as its dominant theme a plea for greater honesty with ourselves and the truth about our failures and our needs.

Short sections deal with various aspects of the spiritual life—Prayer, Penance, Mass, the Sacraments, Our Lady, the Virtues—all showing how our perfection consists not primarily in what we do, but in what we let God do in us.

Here is spiritual reading in a contemporary and adult idiom, a book which may be taken up at the odd five minutes during the day or last thing at night. It is the kind of book that can be re-read until it becomes almost a vade-mecum for any Christian who makes that extra effort to advance in the life of spirit which follows upon *The Choice of God*.

THE CHOICE OF GOD

THE
CHOICE OF GOD

by

Dom Hubert van Zeller

TEMPLEGATE

SPRINGFIELD ILLINOIS

NIHIL OBSTAT: DANIEL DUIVESTEIJN S.T.D.
CENSOR DEPUTATUS

IMPRIMATUR: E. MORROGH BERNARD
VICARIUS GENERALIS

WESTMONASTERII, DIE XXIX MAII, MCMLVI

MADE AND PRINTED IN GREAT BRITAIN
First Published 1956

CONTENTS

PREFACE

TO some this book will appear harsh. They will say that it lacks the spirit of the Gospel. Admittedly the design of life which it proposes is roughed out in straight lines, but so is the Sermon on the Mount. 'It was said to them of old ... but I say to you', and then came stern words. Our Lord distinctly said that 'narrow is the gate and straight is the way that leadeth to life ... not every one that saith to me, Lord, Lord, shall enter into the kingdom of heaven. ... Many will say to me in that day: Lord, have not we prophesied in thy name and cast out devils in thy name and done many miracles in thy name? And then will I profess unto them: I never knew you. Depart from me.' At the end of it St Matthew notes that Christ taught 'as one having power': not as one who made everything easy.

If in this book, then, the matter is found to be not as comforting, and the manner not as tender, as the reader has become accustomed to from the spiritual literature of the past twenty years or so, it is because there is felt to be a need for a less apologetic exposition of the case. The literature of spirituality is getting soft; spiritual people are accordingly getting soft. It is time that souls were reminded that Christ called for penance every bit as forcefully as did John the Baptist. And St John was an ascetic in the direct tradition of the standard model of austerity, Elias.

If Christ, having joy set before Him, chose rather to live hard and die in suffering, then those who try to shape their lives round His can hardly go far wrong in preferring the rugged way of the ancients to the smoother way of the moderns. May they at least be given credit for taking Christ at what they believe to be His word.

The question has been asked by one who has read the book in manuscript whether the lay reader is envisaged or whether

vii

the doctrine is meant properly for monks and nuns. By way of answer it might be suggested that the difference in the spiritual-reading public is not whether the student of books like this present one is in religion or not but whether he seriously pursues the interior life or not. Though intended primarily for those who have the opportunities normally enjoyed by religious for the life of prayer—and certain sections quite obviously apply to those who serve God in this particular way—the book is meant to help also those who, though living in the world, are doing their best to live contemplatively. In other words much of what follows will be useless to the man who objects that after a hard day's work at the office it is a lot to expect that he should deny himself his novel, his television, his cigar. Such a reader would do well to read spiritual books of a lighter kind before he turns to this. The reader envisaged here will not find the truths addressed to the soul repressive—certainly not more repressive than what he finds in St John of the Cross—and it is to be hoped that he will find them light-bringing. But he will have to make the effort to understand them as they are meant to be understood.

A MAN may say 'I choose God', and imagine that from now on the Holy Spirit may be expected to take over. He has meant the choice, and he feels that this is about as much as he can do. Sanctity, he says, will develop out of this as a flower from a bulb. So it will if the man understands the choice as putting God first under all circumstances, in everything, and all the time.

But 'I choose God' may mean one of a variety of things. It may mean: 'Where there is a conflict of claims, I give in to the demand of God.' This is very proper: every Christian has to mean this by implication whenever he says the *Our Father*. At least it guarantees that the man is trying to keep the commandments.

Again the words may mean: 'Where there is a decision to be made, conflict or no conflict, I choose the course which is more likely to further God's interest.' This is an advance on the other. In fact it is the beginning of sanctity and may lead to martyrdom. It is an heroic choice to make, and not all souls should be encouraged to make it in case the decision is found to lead to scruple.

Lastly 'I choose God' may mean this: 'In every creature, in every happening, in every place and pleasure and success and failure, and at every moment of the day and night, I want God to be praised. I want God to get more out of all these things than I do. I want everything to be entirely subject to Him. If necessary I am ready to forgo the pleasure of knowing that what I have just said is the slightest use to Him or to anybody. I choose what He lets me know, what He lets me suffer, what He lets me have for the running of my spiritual and physical life.' A number of people say this kind of thing every day. They read it out of their prayer-books. But very few mean it. If they meant it and were faithful to it they would be saints.

When the saint says 'I choose God' he is really saying 'I am not going to choose any more: my happiness consists in letting God choose.' My will is to do the will of Him who sent me. I

I

live, now not I, but Christ lives in me. I choose, now not I, but Christ chooses for me. I have chosen to be identified with the choice of God.

Is this a shrinking from responsibility? Is it a running away from life—with life's decisions and crises and razor-edged loyalties? No, it is only a shrinking from selfishness—which we have got to shrink from anyway if we would be upright men at all. It is not a running *from* but a running *into*. And once a man has fully committed himself to the choice of God, he does not have to worry overmuch about the choice which denies him the pleasures of creatures.

Election supposes rejection. Not only is this the case in the choice between good and evil, but between good and good. The novice who chooses to aim at the perfection of the Carthusian has to choose not to aim at the perfection of the Franciscan, the Dominican, the Jesuit. The bridegroom who is leading a bride to the altar is refusing to lead any other brides to the altar.

The works of God's hands are good. God says so Himself. But when the soul has fully chosen God, he has chosen absolute Goodness and rejected relative goodness. It so happens that when the selection has been ratified, when God has accepted the soul's goodwill offering, the relative excellences of God come back again and are enjoyed on a different plane. This is what is meant by the hundredfold which is the reward of renunciation. But it is first for the soul to make sure that 'I choose God' is meant literally.

It is not enough, as we have seen, to say 'I choose God' and hope for the best. We must go on meaning it. For one reason or another we can go on for years choosing the recognized symbols of God's will, but it is not so easy to go on choosing God Himself. It is only the love of God that will make us deny ourselves the right to choose anything but God Himself.

Men will always be found in the Church who can do without things for the love of God; men will not so easily be found who can do without their own way of doing things for the love of God.

Perfection is something more than either doing or doing without: it is being. Perfection is choosing to have no will outside the will of God. A snap decision as the result of a crisis is no guarantee of perfection: the choice has to be a constant, a habit. The habit of choosing God is one which is built up in the soul by grace, and in the measure that the habit is preserved the implications of the choice are seen to expand.

'I choose God' is now no longer a formula to be clutched at in moments of emergency: it is the instinctive movement of the soul towards the Creator reflected in His works. 'I choose God' reaches out to every created effect. Equally it reaches in to every experience, emotion, and thought.

Souls who are granted to choose in this way must surely find that the renunciations of the ascetical life cost them little. They are impelled along the way by an energy which is generated inside them. *Caritas Christi urget nos.* I renounce myself, now not I but Christ renounces in me. The ascetical life is, after all, only the fringe of the business: it provides the discipline, the framework, the conditions, the rules. It is the renunciations involved in the mystical life that souls find harder to bear. Harder to bear because harder to see.

But whatever we mean when we say 'I choose God', and however little we realize at the time the implications of our choice, the fact remains that we could not even make the choice at all were it not that God had chosen us first. In electing to become Christ's disciples we are doing no more than ratifying the election as it has stood eternally in His mind.

The important question is not why we choose Him but why He chooses us. Important, but admitting of a perfectly clear answer: He chooses us for the reflexion of Himself which He sees there—for the power which He has given us of shaping our lives according to His. He looks to us for perfection: not our perfection, but His. And because by His grace we can become perfect, He chooses to see us as recipients of His love—as lovable. The God of love cannot but love what He has deemed capable of loving, cannot refuse to love Himself. What He loves in me is what He has put into me of Himself.

3

So when I have done all in my power to serve Him, made the choice and even been faithful to it, am I not still an unprofitable servant? Of myself unprofitable, in Christ magnificently profitable. It is all in the fifteenth chapter of St John's Gospel. 'You have only to live on in me ... if a man lives on in me, and I in him, then he will yield abundant fruit ... it was not you that chose me, it was I that chose you ... the task I have appointed you is to go out and bear fruit, fruit which will endure.'

My perfection consists not in what I do, but in what I let Him do in me. The saint is not one who has begun with nothing and built himself up into a saint. The saint is one who has begun with everything from the moment when he was baptized, and has freely and perfectly yielded to the Christ-life building itself up within him. 'I live, now not I but Christ liveth in me.'

I should not imagine, then, that in making the supremely important choice of my life I am bestowing a benefit upon God. It is not 'I am embracing religion and all that it implies: I am sure God will be very pleased'; it is rather 'God is in this place and I knew it not; I must take off my shoes for I am on holy ground.' Nor is God's attitude towards my choice: 'Here is one who, from among the millions surrounding him, has singled Me out for first place: he must be a very nice person.' It is rather: 'I have favoured this soul, and if he lives up to the grace I am giving him he has the world before him—this world and the next.'

God has called us out of servitude that we may choose what He has chosen for us. 'I do not speak of you any more as my servants; a servant is one who does not understand what his master is about, whereas I have made known to you all that my Father has told me; and so I have called you friends.'

THE whole problem of life is how to respond with the minimum of resistance to the magnet of divine love. All creation is designed to flow back to the Creator from whom it has its being: where this gravitation is denied you have rebellion and sin; where it is accepted and furthered you have—ultimately—sanctity. Sanctity is the willing and loving conformity with God's plan.

Love is the most powerful force in the world, and God is love. Where material things follow the course of a natural law which draws them towards conformity with the pattern as it exists in the mind of God, rational beings are given the chance of helping or hindering the process. Human creatures can tend deliberately towards union with God. That is what they are here for.

Across the wastes and craters and mountains, across the network of roads which claim to lead somewhere but in fact bend back upon their own tracks, the soul has to let itself be drawn by the light which leads to divine union. Love is there, the attraction is there. Even the Person is there to show how the work is to be performed. 'I, if I be lifted up, will draw all things to myself.'

Christ draws. Because He is love He could not fail to draw. But note that in the drawing He is 'lifted up'. He is crucified and magnetic at the same time. The connexion is not accidental but essential. And because like cries out to like, we too—the drawn—have to love, to invite, to reflect the crucifixion.

Perhaps in the whole course of the spiritual life there is no greater light than that which dawns on the first uncertain shape of the love of God. The moment when the soul becomes aware of having a divinely appointed place in the created order, of having an ideal to follow which is beyond ambition, and above all of being an object of God's direct and personal love, is a moment of singular grace. Yes, probably this early consciousness of being related in love is the most far-reaching experience of all.

But what, asks the soul, is the course from now on? Staff in hand, the soul is ready to go anywhere and brave anything. Given a clear directive, the pilgrimage is as good as launched. The commandments? I will put my initials to each of them. The creed and the catechism? Not a clause that I would dream of questioning. The gospel? It is the only ideal I want to follow.

It is not, however, as clear-cut as this. We get our charter given to us in writing. The map is drawn for us on the blackboard. There is always the Church to provide us with the commentaries and the instructions in map-reading. But when we actually start out along the way we discover our loneliness, and this makes us uncertain of ourselves. It is not that we doubt the direction or the validity of the helps provided: it is that we doubt ourselves.

Tell four different men who have never seen the play to get up the part of Hamlet. You will get four different Hamlets. The text, word for word, has been the same for each of them. Take these men to the theatre and show them the part being played by an actor of genius. You will still get four different Hamlets. Not quite as different as before, but still different.

Every man who has been baptized into the body of Christ has got the word of Christ to go by. He has got his mandate. He has even got his model. But within the limits of the text, and in the reproducing of the model, there is an almost infinite variety of interpretation. All that Inspiration can give us, all that the Church can give to us, is a frame of reference. It is within the frame that the likeness to Christ is developed.

We think of the service of God too much as something which we take up. 'I have discovered at last what life is all about', we say, 'so I must now find the right way of fulfilling my destiny: I must go over to religion and take up the study of Christ.' But we must remember that the only reason why we have been granted to discover anything is because God loves us first. The only reason why we have the least leaning towards religion and Christ is because God loves us first.

'You have not chosen me, but I have chosen you.' The

explanation of everything is that God wants us. Allowing that our whole function is to want God back, the way we show our response to love is to let ourselves go on being chosen. All the time we are being the objects of God's choice. And if, again, like cries out to like, our truest life is fulfilled in the act of making God the object of our own choice.

As soon as it has become clear to me that the one great and significant adventure of my life is to go out and find God, I shall see the importance of finding myself. How can I know God if I do not know myself? How can I expect God to come to one who is not sure of his own identity? I do not know enough even of my own nothingness, let alone of the something that God's choice of me calls into being.

I see that all my life I have posed, under one or other of a hundred different disguises, as someone I am not. I realize now, and with dread, that these parts into which I have projected whatever there was of a real self have quite overlaid the person as designed by God, and that I am hidden from the truth about myself.

I tell myself that I must begin again, that I must go back behind the layers of make-up. I must lock myself into a bare room and must study myself from the outside through the keyhole. I must see what I am like when I am not trying to impress either myself or anyone else, when I have nobody from whom to hide. I must catch myself at my most natural, my most true. I do this, and when I look through the keyhole there is nobody there. It is a Henry James conception applied to reality, to my own soul.

Like the man in the H. G. Wells story I am visible only by the clothing that I wear. Take off garment after garment— which is what the spiritual life will do for me anyway later on, and do far more effectively—and there is nothing to see. The person whom I am looking for is out of sight, has vanished.

The reason for all this—this inability to find the true identity which I realize has got to be found if I am to have anything to offer to God—is that I have begun my search from the

7

wrong end. I shall find myself only in finding Christ. If I am to discover myself as I exist in the mind of God, I must be one with the mind of God in the Person of His Son.

As I set myself to serve God I come more and more to realize how vital it is to be true. I see how fatal are these escapes into false selves, into other people's identities, into evasions and stage characters and lay figures. More and more do I come to see that my only hope is to find God who can absorb me into His truth. I am nothing, I am a lie. My humbug can be blown away by the merest puff of His Spirit. So I must come to live in that area where His spirit breathes.

Not only have I never known myself but I may never come to know myself. But I am known to God, and this is evidently enough for Him to work on. Gradually, if I am made strong enough to bear the shame of it, God may make myself known to me in part—prayer burning the grace of humility into me—but the first thing for me to do is to search for Him. Only in His love can I find my true being. He has chosen me: this is the starting point.

THE CONDITION

THOUGH nearly all the laws of the spiritual life are subject to qualification—souls differing so much in their receptivity to grace—the dispositions required of those who want to serve God run pretty much to pattern. And when you examine those dispositions you find that they amount to the same thing.

To begin with you must believe that while you have only the vaguest idea as to the perfection which is proposed to you, and the means which are to be taken to attain it, God has a perfectly clear concept of what He wants from you, and that both as regards the kind of perfection itself and the means which He wants you to take towards realizing it His ideas are certainly different from your own.

8

Next you must have confidence in God's continued desire, your own infidelities notwithstanding, to make you perfect. You must, that is, look more to the constancy of God than at the inconstancy of man. If human nature steadily desires its own happiness, God's desire for the happiness of human nature is no less fixed. And because God wants your happiness more than you do, it is a desire which is more worth counting on than your own.

Lastly you must aim at arriving at that state of mind where God's pleasure, and even other people's pleasure, will become so vital to you that you are not any longer concerned about your own. You must look forward to the sanctity which is self-forgetting rather than to the sanctity which is self-sanctifying.

These are the three conditions for the spiritual life because they are the conditions, in a less specific form, of all religion. They represent the three theological virtues: faith, hope, and charity. Other dispositions, however heroic they appear at first sight, can never provide a foundation on which the life of prayer must be built. The theological virtues *are* the life of prayer.

In order to serve God, then, I have to believe that God's will is the only absolute, and that all else is contingent. More, I have to allow for God's will taking all sorts of contingent turns which seem inconsistent with His absolute will. When this happens I am to remember that His immediate will is the absolute will of God for me.

The contradiction which I endure in the service of a God who apparently has two ways of willing is seen now not as the impact of one force upon another—practical conflicting with the theoretical—but as the fusion of two expressions of divine love in the single immediate grace. It is not that my act of faith disposes of a contradiction but that God's act of love disposes of my doubt.

So much for the disposition corresponding to theological faith. The disposition corresponding to hope is best seen in its effects. In my desire to serve God perfectly I must show that I expect the best from Him and not the worst or the moderate.

I must look forward to grace, and not look back at those graces which I have wasted.

This has nothing to do with blind optimism. It has more to do with blind faith. Optimism is sometimes superstition: hope is next in the sequence to faith. Hope is only faith applied to the future. Many people limit both their faith and their hope by mourning what they conceive to be the death of their opportunity. This is often couched in terms of humility but it is as good as saying that the cause of our failure was insufficient grace.

Pride may be confident but it is never strictly hopeful. If hopefulness is one of the conditions of the service of God, humility is no less so. They go together. Pride analyses, measures, selects, sees all things in terms of self and therefore in a looking glass. And because it sees them in a looking glass it sees them inverted. Humility throws open the gates, takes everything for granted. Nothing piece-meal in the self-forget-fulness of humility and hope.

If I am to serve God well, then, I must begin from a knowledge of my worthlessness and stretch out to the highest that my hope can take me. I must hope with an open and all-embracing hope. The more I focus my hope on particular benefits, the more I restrict the area of my service.

Say I go on a private pilgrimage to Lourdes expecting a particular favour and deciding to attend those devotional exercises which appeal to me. 'I am more recollected this way' I tell myself, 'and I shall be able to concentrate on the intention for which I am praying.' At the end of it I may or may not have gained the favour, but I have not gained much else. My dispositions for serving God are probably no better than they were before. Say I take the alternative course, not visiting Lourdes on my own but coming all the way with others, the chances are that my soul will be wide open to grace even before I start, and that from every angle new graces will flow in. Services, discomforts, emotional transports and desolations, meals, fellow pilgrims—all swept up together and taken as part of the enterprise. This is because I have hoped, not for a single benefit, but for all benefits. Or rather I have taken benefits for granted and have been ready for whatever might come. My 'intention', because universalized, has been granted. Not having identified Lourdes in my mind with what I could get but with what I could offer, I have given greater glory to God than I could have given by making a more personal and recollected pilgrimage. My 'open hope' has been rewarded. It is just such an open hope that I shall need if I am to dispose myself for the life-time service of God.

Lastly there is the disposition which reflects the theological virtue of charity. In order to begin at all in the fullest service of God, the soul must propose to itself the life of love. The life of high love and real love this must be, not merely the forced upright behaviour of the one who is content to act on strict principle. The soul must desire to give to overflowing.

Here it is no longer a question of what is due to God from the creatures which He has made, no longer a question of whether rational human beings have rights of their own: it is a question of what *this* creature *can* offer to Him, of what *this* rational human being *can* possibly find to give.

As in divine love, so in human love: it is the ideal that is proposed, not the duty. And the ideal in natural relationship, as in the supernatural, is found in sacrifice. Self-giving is the only test, the only expression, the only means. Where this ideal is lowered—whether to meet either the standards of the world or the failures of the individual soul—the disposition towards charity suffers.

Charity presupposes understanding and sympathy and regard for the supernatural destiny of every other created soul. How can these qualities which are presupposed be expressed if the quality which presupposes them is understood only as the world understands it ? If the world sees love in terms of desire it has not begun to see what charity is all about. And if religious people see charity in terms of having the unfortunate adequately provided for they have not begun to see what love is all about.

Just as man's love for God suffers on the one hand from the rigid systems of the theorist and on the other from the false pieties of the sentimentalist, so man's love for man is equally found to suffer from being too coldly forced on the one hand and too freely released on the other.

If human relationships are to be proof against the applied charity which chills and turns away, and also against the opposite extreme which burns with false affection and thus justifies the cynical view of love which is held in the world, they must be securely founded in the love which is taught by Christ. What with the inhibitions and evasions of the devout, and the frank mockery of the indevout, it is a wonder that human love is served as well as it is.

Unless human relationships know the true meaning of *compassio* and *congaudeo* they can be no foundation for supernatural charity. It is only the man of faith who can be the man of charity. The man of no faith who loves another can be loving at best only a part of himself which he sees reflected in that other person; at worst he is loving a satisfaction which he feels he is able to get from that other person. It is impossible to love a person simply 'for that person's sake'. Always there is a shadow across the face. Nearly always it is our own shadow. Happy are we, and happy too is that other person, if the shadow is God's.

If then the truly lovable quality in human beings is hidden from the man who has no knowledge of God, it follows that the more a man prays and develops his knowledge of God the more will he come to see what is worth loving in other people. And the more, too, will he be prepared to purify the love which he knows to be imperfect. He will both see more than what he sees and love better what he loves.

Under the influence of the spiritual life the faculty of love, at once the most excellent and the most dangerous thing in the world, will be co-ordinated and directed. Never quite secure, it will, so far as is possible in this life, be safeguarded. In the case of the saints human love becomes absorbed into divine love, finding its expression again in true human charity.

If false love can turn men into animals, true love can turn men into saints. We hear this platitude so often that we never trouble to take it to bits and reassemble it with our own hands. But this is what we should do with all the truths of religion. Truth is no less to be developed because it happens to be a truism.

Christ's love of souls must be shared by us. He loves people not on principle but because they are by Him made lovable. The fact that in many cases we have to take this on faith in no way lessens the love which we should be able to show towards those whom He loves and in whom He dwells. These people *are* lovable. And if we aspire to the loving service of God we must know that to search for the lovable in others, and to love truly when we have found it, is an essential in that service.

Also it makes all the difference to the way in which we serve. The *compassio* which is the fruit of obligation is a cold hard fruit. It needs to be ripened with rays of charity from the heart or it will wither on the stem. Do you never have to listen to the troubles of someone who does not at all attract you? What happens? You deliver your piece of sympathy at the end of the recital, but it comes from the sternly commanding will. It may help the troubled soul—you hope it will—but it cannot reach the marrow, it is a tepid oil flowing slowly. Compare this with what happens when you listen to much the same story from one for whom you feel an affection. You long to share the burden, you can hardly wait to make the offer, you go to any lengths afterwards to help.

If natural love can transform the scene in the dramas of natural relationship, supernatural love can equally transform supernatural service. Love is the whole aim, love is the completely transfiguring miracle, love is the one sole explanation. It must be on this bedrock foundation, in intention at least, that the whole structure of God's service must rest.

13

FOR the man who plans to walk in the footsteps of Christ there have to be certain separations which the world—which even the majority of confessors—would judge to be unnecessary and excessive.

In a great number of cases the call to sanctity demands the change from one state of life to another. In a still greater number of cases it requires those summoned to stop on in the state of life in which they are. Sometimes, but not often, you find souls who seem to be called by God to make many alterations in their state of life. They make the change, and then after a while they have to begin all over again with another change. But although they may find their sanctity in this—indeed must find their sanctity in it—the precedent is not one which we may safely follow. That arrangement of life which seems to have no arrangement is beyond legislating for: it has to come under a more direct handling of the Holy Spirit.

Of the three vocations perhaps the hardest is the one which is worked out on the flat—in the original condition of life without any outward change at all. It is hard because since there has to be an alteration of some sort, the alteration is interior and so all the more painful. Interior transformations are involved in the other two vocations as well, but at least here there is the framework of the new life to help.

No sooner does a man decide to aim at high holiness than he will be told by his friends two things: first, not to take himself too seriously; second, not to burn his boats. Both these ideas are contradicted in the gospel.

The would-be saint, eager to become a fool for Christ's sake, is asked to keep his sense of proportion. The willing burner of boats is told he may by all means set fire to the luxury fittings but that he would be wise to leave the craft intact in case there are journeys to be made later on. The one thing the man wants is not to be wise any more. The foolish has God chosen to confound the wise.

So long as there is thought of a possible return to the wisdom of the world, to the strength of the world, to the standards and pleasures and deceptions of the world, there is a pull in the wrong direction. The soul cannot concentrate. It is not a question of sin being the great attraction. There is perhaps no specified attraction at all. It is simply that the door is left open and there is a draught. There is nothing so distracting as a draught.

The gospel is all for making a decision and abiding by it. It is the only way to peace. The soul is asked to make up its mind on three points. First, is this thing a good in itself—is it of God? Second, is it the kind of thing which is good for me—is it what God is offering to me personally? Third, can I, with God's help, follow the thing through to the end? If the answer is 'Yes' to each question, then the sooner he goes about it the better. He has found, or has begun to find, his vocation.

Nor should all this be taken as applying to vocation in the strict sense: it applies to any project or opening which requires of the soul a serious decision. The married state, no less than the single or the religious, needs to be embarked upon in terms of Gospel discipleship. But it is not the married state that is specifically considered here. The present purpose is to find principles which may guide the soul towards union with God. And the first of these is that a man should not leave himself a peep-hole through which to look back.

Even if there is no intention of going back, the mere act of looking back is a thoroughly bad thing. It stores up images which the memory will feed upon later on. Memory is more of a trouble than it is given credit for. Even if we cannot ever fully eliminate the harmful effects of memory, we can do something towards starving it out. We can remove the objects on which it delights to fasten.

To allow the mind to dwell upon material which is outside the scope of the call from God is to go far towards providing excuses for ultimately reclaiming what has been renounced. Once the singleness of the original purpose is lost, the soul will find itself turning round and round. It loses its direction. The hand on the plough is uncertain: the furrow begins to waver away from the straight.

The only way to avoid the distraction of feeling that I want to turn round is to have something really worth while to look at in front of me. 'I have lifted up my eyes to the mountains, from whence shall help come to me.' So it is really more a question of keeping my vision fixed than of keeping a smoke-screen at my heels. But if I become scornful of smoke-screens I shall find myself becoming doubtful about mountains. I shall begin to mistake my mountain for a mirage.

'He will steer my feet clear of the hunter's trap.' He, God, will take care of my feet: all I have to do is to direct my face towards Him. If my face is truly set I need have no further hesitations. The psalmist says that the man of God must forget his father's house. Christ Himself says that the neophyte may not go home to comfort his parents. Then comes the voice of the world, and we are told that it is only prudent to allow for possible changes of circumstances later on. The world plays for a certain kind of safety. It does not play for faith.

'Yes,' you will say, 'but how about the man who started to build a tower and had afterwards to leave off? How about the king who went to war and then found that he had not enough men?' The answer is that neither had counted the cost. In the business of vocation we are dealing here with souls who have weighed up the consequences. Those who build or go to war on sudden impulse will learn their mistake: we are not now worrying about the hair-trigger enthusiasts. It is the serious, deliberate, circumspect response to grace that is the subject-matter of this book.

IMMEDIATE RENUNCIATIONS

IN following any treatment of this subject it must be remembered at every point that the whole purpose of asceticism is to free the soul for the further advance towards God. Renunciations are positive or they are nothing. Indeed they are unitive or they are nothing. We give things up that we may the better give. We deny ourselves because Christ denied Himself. Penance is fruitful only because of, and in the measure that it is united to, the Passion.

Perhaps because of the present generation's increased nervous sensibility, or perhaps as a reaction against the particularized systems of mortification which were taught in an earlier age, penance is not given much of a hearing to-day. It is, however, difficult to see how a man may get nearer to God if he is scornful of the detachments which have been insisted upon until the spiritual writers found excuses for evading them.

We do not have to meditate upon the justice and anger of God if we would form principles by which we can direct our ascetical life: it is quite enough to meditate upon His love and His mercy. The more we learn about divine love the more we see the need for personal mortification. It is not Jansenist to feel that we must be serious about our renunciations; it is severely Catholic.

Humanity, you will protest, is right and good. If nature is crushed, renounced at every turn, there is a waste. Man has been given his appetites by God, and they cannot all be wrong. It seems so uncomplimentary to God to get rid of the legitimate pleasures which He has put into this world for our enjoyment.

That sort of thing can be strung out indefinitely. And it is not easy for the uninspired upholder of penance to answer. Let Inspiration then provide the argument. 'Thus, brethren,' says St Paul to the Romans, 'nature has no longer any claim upon us, that we should live a life of nature. If you live a life of nature you are marked out for death; if you mortify the ways of nature through the power of the Spirit you will have life.' And a few verses later: 'We are children of God ... only we must share His sufferings if we are to share His glory.'

Thus whether the summons to holiness demands a change of state or not, the demand to mortify the natural man is absolute. The first obligation is to clear from the margins of life those creatures or pleasures or desires which h ave no bearing upon

17

the service of God. For the straight choice of God the soul must be unencumbered.

Allowing that a man is confident that he is in the condition of life which is willed for him by God, he has to distinguish between those satisfactions which are of the essence of his vocation and those which are not. He must then get rid of the collateral ones. Though a man be called to live a life of sanctity in the world, he is not to imagine that this entitles him to use the world's amusements.

Nor, for the matter of that, may the man who is called to live the life of sanctity in religion assume that the relaxations which happen to be provided by his particular religious order are to be indiscriminately enjoyed.

The world supplies, and religious orders supply, a rich variety of recreations. It is for the soul to find out which, for him, are necessary and which are idle. The test will lie in his honest reading of the word 're-creation'. Recreations which do not mean a renewal of spiritual energy are dissipations. If the object is to re-create, it is no compensation to re-distribute. By a false use of recreation, interests and appetites which have been mortified at the first conversion are found to revive and multiply: they become newly directed towards a variety of secondary ends.

Neither the liberties nor the renunciations, then, are exactly defined by the state of life. The state of life gives no more than an indication. If smoking, television, radio, wine, films and plays are ill suited to the saint in religion, they are scarcely less ill suited to the saint in the world. Saints renounce these things as unnecessary. Saints may on occasion be forced into using them, and when this happens they do so with reserve, but the recreation of the saints is not to be found in worldliness.

The man who allows himself such luxuries as are mentioned above either needs them—in which case they are necessities to him—or he does not. If he needs them it means that his physical, nervous, and mental constitution should be trained to a better independence. If he does not need them they are a self-indulgence and should be dropped.

Let us come out into the open about this. Can men who seriously call themselves disciples of Christ, who look upon the lives they lead as being genuinely religious, allow themselves to smoke, drink, and spend time on entertainment?

'But if Christ were living to-day, would He not grant His disciples these harmless relaxations?' He probably would. He almost said as much: 'Shall the children of the marriage fast as long as the bridegroom is with them?' But the whole point is that since He spoke those words He has died on the cross because of our sins. 'When the bridegroom shall be taken away, then shall they fast in those days.' If the Bridegroom were present in Person to-day we would be justified in celebrating. But since His death His disciples no longer enjoy the dispensations granted at weddings.

The follower of Christ ought not to need for his recreation (in the sense denoted) more than what his mind and senses in the ordinary way supply. He should not have to step out of the ordinary limits set by his vocation in order to enjoy himself. Provided he can read, can use his hands, can see and taste and hear the more or less pleasurable things that come along— provided he keeps awake to these things of course—he ought to be able to manage. What more in the way of external satisfactions should the man of God expect?

To be pledged to the service of God is to be pledged to simplicity of life. If those who so pledge themselves neglect to canalize their interests, they must inevitably feel the need for frivolous indulgence. Human nature, never quite sure about happiness, craves anyway to be entertained. We are prepared to shelve the question of true joy so long as we can be kept amused. But if the supply of entertainment is cut off, we find that human nature is quite satisfied to get along with the more lasting satisfactions provided by work. It is for the man of prayer to discover interests which will act as substitutes for amusements.

But if the follower of Christ is not strong enough to do without newspapers, television, novels, parties and so on, then for goodness' sake let him be honest about it and confess them to

19

be weaknesses. Let us have no nonsense about his state of life making them almost a duty. If a man must beguile himself with worldly entertainments—be they printed, recited, sung, served on a plate, poured from a decanter, or taken out of a box—then he had better keep quiet about reasonable outlets which must be allowed to a body and brain habitually employed in the service of God.

Cant and humbug run clean contrary to the life of prayer. And nowhere do you find more of it than among religious people. It is better to accuse yourself of weakness, and to ask God for greater generosity, than to count yourself generous and make excuses for being weak. The life of prayer is the life of truth. It is untrue to say that you need not, under the circumstances, renounce yourself: it is not untrue to say that you cannot, under the circumstances, bring yourself to.

If the man of the world and the man of God share the same amusements, follow the same interests, have the same standards of living, what is the difference between them? If mortification means anything at all it must mean the denial of the non-essential. Certain appetites must be starved so that certain other appetites may be nourished. The vine must be dressed, the sapling must be tied to a stick and trained to grow straight.

Oh yes, we all know that it is possible to enjoy pruning the vine for the sake of the pruning and not for the sake of the vine. Oh yes, we all know that some people naturally prefer to be tied to a stick than to be allowed to grow up on their own. We can become wedded to a penance or a system of penance just as we can become wedded to an indulgence or an excuse for indulgence. But this does not destroy the need for a carefully devised policy of renunciation.

If I am a drunkard I have to deny myself the pleasures of drink. This is obvious enough. But not so many people after all are drunkards. Everybody, or nearly everybody, likes listening to music, staying in bed, wearing good clothes, eating properly cooked food. There is plenty of scope for mortification among those of us who are not drunkards.

'Yes,' you may say, 'but to drink to excess is wrong; it is not wrong to enjoy the wireless, to sleep the full eight hours, to dress and eat well.' All right then it is not wrong. And nobody is asking you to give up all but the minimum of sleep, food, and clothing. What you are being asked to give up is all that you *can* give up. And that for the love of God.

Throughout this chapter, as throughout this book, it must be insisted that we are not considering what is permissible but what is perfect; not what a soul has to do for peace of conscience, but what it may do for love of God. If only people would search the Scriptures for confirmation of their wild hopes, and not for justification of their tame lives, they would be a good deal happier and the world would come nearer to practising the Sermon on the Mount.

'No man can serve two masters ... he that shall lose his life for me shall find it ... if thou wilt be perfect, go sell what thou hast and give to the poor and come follow me ... whosoever does not carry his cross and come after me cannot be my disciple.' It is all there, in the Gospel. What we need are directors and preachers who will see with the single eye, who will point the straight way, who will invite to the unqualified choice of God.

PRAYER AND ART

THE poet who is too poetic cannot produce good poetry. The same principle applies to each of the arts. If an actor is more an actor than he is a person, he not only loses sight of the individual whom he is meant to be but also fails to express true drama. The painter, the composer, the dancer: each must discover for himself the point at which, if he goes any farther, he loses touch with his essential purpose.

At once you ask, 'Do you mean his essential purpose as a man or as an artist?' The answer is 'Both'. The purpose of the artist and the purpose of the rational being are the same. The artist differs from his fellows only in his vocation to unveil the beauty which he, together with the rest of mankind, must refer back to Beauty Itself.

Granted that all men are intended to see in created beauty a reflexion of God, and that some men see this less clearly than others, and that some do not see it at all, the vocation of the artist is in a sense an apostolate. It is for him to give sight to the blind.

The artist is the one who has always got one lens more in his telescope than the ordinary man. He sees the heavens, and must explain them to others. This, whether he knows it or not and whether he likes it or not, is his function.

If the artist collaborates with God, uniting his creative art with the creative act of God, he will be a good man and probably a good enough artist. If he refuses to work with God—that is to say if he insists on creating independently of Him whom he recognizes as Creator—then he will not be a good man, nor, in the strictest sense, a good artist. In his rebellion against the source of truth and beauty, the artist may still show great talent and even genius. But he will fail in the one thing for which his power has been given him. He will be rendering no service to truth and beauty.

The artist who knows God's purpose regarding art and defies it is like any other anarchist, any other heretic: in denying the order which is of God, he destroys the person which is himself. In trying to become more of an artist and less of a servant of God, he may become more of an individualist but he will become less of an individual. It is sad to watch promising artists deteriorate and turn out to be, in the literal sense, non-entities.

Truth is beauty and beauty is truth. This is all the artist knows and all he needs to know. If he fails truth he betrays beauty. And in that case there is no particular point in his pretending to be an artist any longer.

It is not only by expressing untruth and ugliness that an artist goes against his vocation. It is not even by expressing nothing at all, wrapping his talent in the napkin of laziness or false humility, that the artist sins. The most common failure of the artist lies in his mania for the expression of self to the exclusion of things more worth expressing.

Where the main consideration is self, what can prevent the finished work of art from being mannered? If the artist's desire rises no higher than the personal adulation he receives, or the sensation he creates, then his gift is not being used as a revelation but as an advertisement.

The straining after effect is death to true art. Cleverness, technical competence, originality: these qualities do not of themselves guarantee true art. There is all the difference in the world between artistry and art.

What the above has been leading up to is this. The religious man, no less than the artistic man, can fail in his profession by being too professional. Just as the artistic can be the enemy of art, so religiosity can be the enemy of religion.

The man of prayer can all too easily be beglamoured by an *expertise* of spirituality which has nothing to do with the true service of God. The service of God is a serious business, more serious than the service of art, and to make merely a culture out of it is to go far towards making mockery of God.

Art and religion seem to have this in common, that they attract the dilettante. The engineer is not as a rule a dabbler; nor is the soldier, the historian, the explorer, the scientist. But in art and religion we tend to follow too much our own taste and impulse to the neglect of reality.

Nor is it only a question of the form which our fastidiousness takes in matters of religion—such as a flair for certain schools of spirituality, a cult of certain aspects of the liturgy, an observance of certain ascetical practices—but, and perhaps more generally, there is the danger of our being smothered by legalism. The light of the spirit can be extinguished by the very laws of the spirit. Laws are designed to bring light and life. It is we who turn them inside out so that they bring darkness and death.

The man of prayer, like the man of art, can bury his head in a desert of formula. He can make it his whole business to

23

perfect himself in things that are secondary. There is in fact no greater obstacle for the religious man than precisely this tendency to mistake the means for the end. The history of both mysticism and asceticism is witness to the tragedy of false emphasis.

The letter of the law, wrongly applied, does not merely waste an energy which might otherwise relate directly to God: it kills it. Life comes from the spirit, and if the spirit is stifled by the letter which is intended to minister to the spirit, the fruit of the spirit is stillborn.

The way to God has been so carefully and elaborately charted that we sit spellbound before the chart. Not before God but before the chart. It is not even that we are afraid to explore the country of God: it is simply that, hypnotized, we are kept in our seats by the chart. The only thing that will uproot us and send us on our way is the conviction that union with God is the one sole reason why we are confronted with a chart at all. But even this conviction, which no sane person would disown if he gave the thing a moment's thought, is not enough to uproot some of us.

We become saints, not by picking our way delicately between the prohibitions of the law, but by stretching out boldly in the direction of love. Just as the only way to love is to keep the law, so the only way to keep the law is to love.

Fear, precision, knowledge of the commentaries will not perfect us in the law. Love will perfect us in the law. Prayer will perfect us in the law. The law without love is a dead thing. It is as dead a thing as prayer would be without God.

Just as the rules and tricks of the art-school can be the most cramping influence when the painter goes out on his own to paint, so the system can be cramping when the soul sets out to love. Nothing so hinders the soul in prayer as the misgiving that the method which looked so good in the book is not being followed. Distractions about food and work are trivial compared with the distraction of remembering and applying the rules for the avoidance of distractions.

If the artist has to shake himself free of the egotism which will always try to dominate his work, of the sentimentality which will cheapen it, of the preoccupation with slogans and doctrinaire principles which will impinge upon his spontaneity, so also has the man of prayer to expose and renounce the same attachments if he is to aim at gospel perfection. The interior soul will never be rid of this selfishness unless he be born again in spirit and in truth—unless he be born again in Christ.

BORN AGAIN

INSTINCTIVELY we think of the spiritual life as something which rises from the ashes. We would do better to think of it as bursting from the bud. Dying to sin and to creatures is important; but not so important as being born again to grace.

The mystery of death is easier for the mind to grasp than the mystery of birth. We can understand the decree that appoints all men to die; we can not so readily understand the decree that appoints some to be born and others not.

In the spiritual order the death to sin and the awakening to grace can be understood in the same act. 'You have undergone death' says St Paul to the Colossians, 'and your life is hidden away now with Christ ... you must be quit of the old self, and the habits that went with it; you must be clothed in the new self that is being refitted all the time.'

We have seen in the foregoing chapter that the man who plies his trade as an artist must abstract from the on-paper lessons, and make straight for what the master who taught him had, or should have had, in mind to reveal. Now just as there comes a stage in the artist's life when he must be born again to the primaries, so there comes a stage in the life of the religious man where a similar rebirth is required. But the religious man has to be reborn in Christ.

25

In his effort to propose to himself Christ and nothing but Christ, the religious man may feel that he would be greatly helped if he could forget all that he had ever read about perfection and prayer—and even about God. Though there may be error lurking in such a thought—since illuminism fastens on this kind of mood—it might be a good thing sometimes to leave the authorities alone and make straight for the study of our Lord.

Allowing that our man does not fall into heresy during the first week, the experiment will at least have the merit of getting him to start at the right end. Ordinarily we start from the wrong end, ourselves, and work towards the knowledge of Christ. So of course we spend longer in the mud than we need. Some people never get out of the mud at all: they are still studying themselves.

We read our Lord's words to Nicodemus, 'a man cannot see the kingdom of God without being born anew', and what do we do? Immediately we turn to the shelves and consult the authorities. This may be partly to show our goodwill, partly to amass as much information as possible on what is obviously a most vital subject, and partly because we are afraid of missing something which was conveyed to Nicodemus but which has not been so clearly conveyed to us.

For most of us when we read the Nicodemus story, or when we read those passages in the epistles which stress the newness of life which is found in Christ, the questions instantly presenting themselves are 'What must I do? Where do I start? How do I behave?' We do not, as we ought to, say frankly 'Show me Christ'.

In order to see Christ we must sometimes stand back not only from creatures but from theories about creatures. We must get above those reasons and experiences and speculations which, though they may point to Christ, cluster so thickly that they hedge Him about and interfere with our sight of Him.

Like Zacchaeus, who 'was trying to distinguish which was Jesus but could not do so because of the multitude', we must 'run on in front and climb up into a sycamore tree'. The crowds are telling us too much; their enthusiastic pointing confuses us; we must get onto a branch and sit there.

All people, but particularly religious people, tend to make too much of religion's details and not enough of religion's essentials. Since the fall we live among shadows and are shy of substance. Are not the devout often more at home among their devotions than among the members of Christ's mystical body?

Invariably the charge against religious people is that of hypocrisy: they are so bent upon the supernatural that they scorn, or forget about, the natural. They hide behind their supposed virtue and condemn the rest. They sort out the minutiae to their satisfaction, and leave unfulfilled the law of love.

Granted that there are many such—many who swallow the camel and strain at the gnat, who make a great business about motes in the eyes of others while there are beams in their own— there are even more unconscious hypocrites in religion who have not the least idea that our Lord is attacking them.

The people who need most to be born again are those who do not recognize its necessity: those who think they have been. These are the people whom their brethren should be praying for.

The real hypocrite, who knows all along that he is a hypocrite, deserves what he gets. There is guilt too in the kind just mentioned—the entrenched but unaware. But there is another kind of religious person who, though not a hypocrite in the absolute sense, is so wedded to his observances that even with the best will in the world he cannot enter into the liberty of the children of God. The truth is he has not got such a good will as he thinks he has. If he had, he would be free. As it is he is a hypocrite. A poor hypocrite, but a hypocrite nevertheless.

Lastly there are those who are not hypocrites at all but who are nevertheless fettered by the externals of religion. Either their training has been wrong or they are by nature inclined to the superficial. These people have no great opinion of themselves, do not parade their observances, and would like to help others. But they seem to make no progress in the service of

God. Their externalism is their escape from reality. And so, in a measure, from God.

At least these last two groups appreciate the need for a re-birth, but they are muddled. They would be less muddled if they prayed more. They would get the light to see how to set about it. And if they corresponded with the light, God would do the rest for them. But people do not pray enough, so of course they go on in the things that stand to them for prayer. We cannot go all the way on a symbol.

The Church makes use of symbols, the saints make use of symbols. Symbols represent and express love, but they are not a substitute for love. Love is an absolute, and there is no substitute for love. Love is an absolute, and there is no substitute for an absolute. Not even suffering is a substitute. Suffering can be the seal of love, and love can be the cause of suffering, but they are not the same thing. 'Love is the fulfilment of the law'; suffering is not.

It is not the Church's fault, nor the gospel's fault, that the law is misinterpreted and that people continue to live in symbols. It is because people do not pray enough, and so do not see what the law is all about.

If people prayed more, and particularly those people whose office it is to pray and to teach the law and to give an example of love, there would be light enough in the world by which the frame of religion could be distinguished from the essence of religion. The essence of religion is Christ, and Christ is love.

'If you love me,' says Christ, 'keep my commandments.' The law must be loved as representing God's will. It is by know-ledge of the law that we come to know God's designs for us; it is by fidelity to the law that we respond to the summons of love. The law, like prayer, is the living channel of correspond-ence between the soul and God. The law, like prayer again, can govern every instant of our day. In such a service as this the law *is* prayer. To such a soul as this the law is a living voice.

But that is exactly what the law is meant to be to everybody:

28

a living voice. If it is not to me a living voice, the only alternative is that it is to me a dead letter. Can I be governed every instant of my day by a dead letter? How can I learn about life from something which is dead? How can I model myself on the portrait when I have only the frame to go by?

If no amount of frames can make a picture and no amount of laws can make a saint, the only course to take is to search for the Model Man, Christ, and to learn from His Spirit how to quicken the letter of the law. This is the start towards being born again. This is the walk across Jerusalem by night in the company of Nicodemus. At least we have our question ready, and we know where to look for the answer.

Though a man may not be able to re-enter his mother's womb, he can go back a long way: he can start from his infancy. In fact unless he is ready to become a child he will not enter into the kingdom of heaven. To get back behind the sophistication of the world, to repudiate the independence and case-hardened maturity of the grown-up, is the best way to dispose yourself for the wisdom of the spirit. You have to be a fool if you are to be wise—with the fortunate foolishness of very young children.

The history of sanctity bears out the paradox that in going back you make your greatest advance. As you retreat from the world's learning, which is full of evasion and deceit, you find yourself being educated by the gospel.

'Yes,' you say, 'I would like to return to the original simplicity of the gospel, but everything in the regimentated society of to-day militates against it.' The desire for an altered setting in which to work out the problem of human happiness and salvation is not the property of religion. Fairy stories, ballets, and at least one opera have provided their various answers to the sighing of the human soul which says 'give me a new start'.

It is in the service of God itself, and not in the alteration of the sphere in which God is served, that the desire to begin again can be met.

Take the man who feels blocked by his work, misunderstood by his family, handicapped by his mistakes. He sees himself a social, and perhaps a moral, failure; he is disillusioned, and talks about being the victim of circumstances. For him, as for the devout humbug, the only solution is to be born again.

It is no good for this man to take his environment to bits and set it up again somewhere else. He has got to take his conscience to bits and set it up again in the same place. To find peace he does not have to change his job or his neighbourhood or his wife: he has to change himself. Or rather he has to exchange himself for Christ.

A dog that is sick may imagine that if only he can extract a splinter that happens to be in his paw all will be well. So a man may identify his unhappiness with his setting. He takes out the splinter and is still sick.

The unsettled, the lonely and obsessed, the millions of men and women who hunger for something and are surprised when a material world leaves them hungrier still, are spiritually sick. What they want is not a reshuffle of outward pressures but a reshuffle of inward values. Not a bonfire of existing effects, but an examination, by the light of the spirit, of primary causes.

For the individual soul, as for this lunatic world as a whole, the cure lies in the response to grace: in the recognition of the will of God. It is not even a question of behaviour—still less a question of economics or geography or social welfare or medicine or therapy—it is a question of being born again in Christ.

LOSING AND FINDING LIFE

A CONCLUSION arising out of the previous section is that the important thing is not so much what a man does but how far he accepts the work as coming from God, and how far he is ready to direct it back again to Him. He must value what he is engaged upon, not according to the intrinsic good of the work, but according to the power of the work to convey to him God's will. And all works, provided they are not of set purpose directed away from God, can convey to us God's will.

Another conclusion is that we are not like children who are told to build a certain kind of house and who are given the wrong sort of blocks to do it with. Infallibly we are given the right sort of blocks. And having used the right ones till the roof of the house is almost on, we are not to say, 'I would have been happier building a bridge.'

All of us yearn for certainty in our vocation, and some of us never find it. We imagine that the security which promised so well in the beginning must be waiting for us, but when shall we be allowed to come into our own? Are we, forever unanchored, to drift through life with no sort of certainty that what we have chosen is what God has chosen for us?

The peace which God wants for us *is* waiting for us, and it is our fault that there has been the delay. It has been there all the time on our doorstep, but we have never fulfilled the conditions for possessing it. A man must lose his life if he will find it. The seed must die first before it can live. A man begins to know his happiness only when he has turned his back on what he thinks it is.

The restless searcher has to die to the good which is apparent if he is to live to the good which is God's. The whole problem for the devout man is to find out in prayer which is which.

The restless searcher has at least this to guide him: he may assume that the work which he happens to be doing is, unless the contrary is clearly shown, the one which God wants him to perfect. If God wants him to leave off building houses and build bridges instead, He will indicate His will. It must not be the soul's rough guess. It would be better even to go on being restless building the houses that God wanted him to build than to be contented and settled building his own bridge.

I would rather spend my life in the wrong box by God's will than in the right one by my own.

Their friends say of the maladjusted, the misfits, that they have never really lived. The truth is that they have never really died.

It is sad to come across instances where spirituality has failed to bring about order and settlement in a soul. Though there is no guarantee that religious souls will feel comfortable in the setting provided for them by God, they should at least enjoy a sense of belonging. 'I may not like it, but it is right.'

Dying in order to live, then, is a matter of surrendering to the conditions lovingly imposed by a loving God. It is yielding to the mould. Nor is this mould the hard mask which stifles, but the flexible mask which has been personally designed to fit our particular face. If we accept it, breathe and look and talk and *think* through it, we become saints.

The saint is only the one who wears the mask so well that he becomes it. Then is he truly in the image and likeness of God. Then has he 'put on Christ'. Then does he 'walk in Christ'. Through the mask which he becomes, and which becomes himself, the saint inhales and exhales the spirit of Christ. He views the world and people through the eyes of Christ, thinks and works and speaks and loves with the mind of Christ.

If on the other hand we resist the mould, hardening ourselves against the touch of grace and shrinking back into our loneliness and misery and independence, we are condemning ourselves to be without life. We are condemning ourselves to hell on earth.

Once we surrender we are no longer wrenched apart: the conflict stops and we are one thing within. Once we surrender we find ourselves being carried across the deserts of anomaly, unreason, injustice. 'When a man becomes a new creature in Christ' says St Paul to the Corinthians, 'his old life has disappeared, everything has become new about him. This, as always, is God's doing; it is he who, through Christ, has reconciled us to himself.'

How far this life-after-death while still on earth is strictly mystical it would be difficult to say. And anyhow it is a question of terms, and is of no consequence. The point is that it uproots us from our shallow securities, which are no securities, and plants us in the power of God. At last we can mean it when we say, 'The Lord is my strength'.

If the Lord really is my strength I can do all things in Him who strengthens me. Even without seeing into the purposes of His mind, I can act in the power which is His will. I do not have to worry about my lack of wisdom: I am brought to participate in His.

'The spirit you have now received is not, as of old, a spirit of slavery to govern you by fear' says St Paul to the Romans, 'it is the spirit of adoption which makes us cry out Abba, Father. The Spirit himself thus assures our spirit that we are the children of God. And if we are his children then we are his heirs too; heirs of God, sharing the inheritance of Christ. Only we must share his sufferings if we are to share his glory.'

No miracle has been performed: exteriorly everything goes on as before. We remain the same variable, moody, sensitive beings, subject to spasms of fear and loneliness. But the disturbances now are superficial, the blunders are taken in the stride. Compare the man facing his dread in a spirit of faith with the man who faces dread without faith.

To know that God has taken us on, has taken the whole of our strain, has got us fitted into the pattern of His life, is to know peace. *This* is security. The secret is open to all. You would think everyone would know it who had read the Passion.

It is in surrender that we discover not only God, our true selves, our peace, but we discover also our true relation to one another: we discover charity. Our human personalities, hampered by the effects of original sin in the first place and thereafter never quite understanding the meaning of life, start off in the service of God at a disadvantage. Until we die to self and begin to live we are disintegrated beings. Charity has not found its proper place in us.

'Created nature,' says St Paul again, 'has been condemned to frustration.' But when God 'who through Christ has reconciled us to himself' has remodelled our lives, re-forming us in the image of His Son, our charity, hitherto a piecemeal and

33

self-regarding duty, is expanded and enriched. Re-collected in Christ, we 'minister this reconciliation of his to others'. The charity of the saints is like the charity of God. It *is* the charity of God.

It is nature that is reflex in its kindnesses to others. The kindness that derives from pure love is as open as the sky, as unselfconscious as the air.

And at any moment this new life is ours for the asking. It is already there, from the moment of our baptism, but we have never made it new. With Nicodemus we have the power of coming out from Christ's presence with the light which will see us through the darkest streets of our journey. 'You must think of yourselves as dead to sin,' we hear so often during the Easter season, 'and alive with a life which looks towards God, through Christ Jesus our Lord.'

A DIFFICULTY

THE reader who has followed the argument to the present stage in the book might reasonably be puzzled by the almost magical properties attributed to the combined influence of baptism and the surrender which we have discussed as the second birth. 'The fact remains,' it could be objected, 'that some problems *are* too much for us, and that even the holiest people collapse when strained beyond a certain point.'

In the first place we must take it as true that to the baptized soul, living in Christ by faith, nothing is impossible to endure and nothing is impossible to achieve. And the reason for this is that it is Christ who is enduring, Christ who is achieving. If a man have this faith he can, by the power of God to whom he is united, move mountains.

The life of faith which derives from the grace of baptism is not a sort of trick which a man learns when he happens to come across the idea of following up his baptism by being born again in adult life. The new vistas which open up to the soul spring neither from a superstition nor from an emotional awakening, a 'conversion'. They spring from just what we have said: the life of faith. Only they do not so much *spring*, as from a box, but gradually dawn. They come to light as the result of habitually co-operating with a grace. Faith is a habit.

Thus it would be a mistake to think of surrender as of a peg being withdrawn, letting in a sudden rush of grace which from now on makes everything look right. Rather should we think of it from God's angle instead of from the soul's—as God being always there, taking the weight, and the soul at a given moment yielding to the surrounding element. The image would therefore be of the tide lifting the grounded vessel—the vessel thereafter reiterating its act of yielding at every moment of its voyage. The fact that it is being constantly supported in the water is the implicit reiteration.

Gradually the horizons widen until there is nothing to be seen on every side but only the sea.

So to the detached soul, the soul that is habitually surrendered, problems are never unsurmountable and sufferings are never likely to cause breakdowns. In fact the more a problem is felt to be beyond him, the more such a soul feels dependent upon God. 'Since I can do nothing about this, I am perfectly happy about it: it is out of my hands.' So long as he has his own judgment to go by, the soul knows that there is danger of self coming in.

Sufferings, on the same principle, are never entirely overwhelming. The attitude is one which says, 'I accept this suffering, and as I am coming to the end of my *own* reserves I am perfectly at peace: I know that if more is required of me, God will take over completely and endure it for me and in me.'

A saint, since there is no guarantee that his body will be miraculously strengthened, may *physically* collapse under suffering. But are there any saints who have become nervous wrecks under it? Can we think of a saint losing spirit, going to pieces, because of the cross?

The reason why the saint can bear his trials without being

unnerved by them is not only that he has hope, and that he has the Agony in the Garden more prominently in his mind than the rest of us, and that he means more than we do when he says the *Our Father*, but also that he is better balanced than most men. Grace and the interior life have cleared his head of the prepossessions which dissipate the mental reserves of ordinary worldly people, so he is not so inclined to lose it.

The man of prayer is integrated, his faculties are in order. He is not disturbed because he is nearer than other men to the state of our first parents before the Fall. Adam and Eve were not liable to nervous breakdowns. The holy man's sensibilities may be acute, but he will never be in the condition when something is likely to snap. Habitual yielding to God eliminates snap.

Where there is no resistance there is no clash. It is the impact of one thing upon another that makes for breakages. But where the soul is always yielding to the pressures God sends there is no room for breakage.

God's will acts on the receptive soul not as a cross falling upon taut muscles but as rain falling upon fleece. *Sicut pluvia in vellus.* It is hardly even the meeting of two wills and the subordination of one of them: it is more the union of two wills and the dual operation of one.

Thus the soul of prayer, far from putting on a defensive armour against them, welcomes circumstances as being the reflexion of God's will. Indeed since he has chosen that God's will should be the motive force of his life, they are the reflexions of his own will as well. It is he who has chosen them—with God. They are the rebound of his own throw.

The man of prayer comes then to absorb whatever the created order tells him of God. And it tells him far more than it tells to those who do not pray. Whether the knowledge is learned painfully or pleasurably is immaterial: for him the important thing is to draw the supernatural significance out of the natural forms.

With the man of prayer there is never the complaint that the natural is obscuring the view of the supernatural. He knows

36

too well that if this were happening it would be his fault for seeing in a natural light things that were meant to be seen supernaturally. To be hampered by temporal affairs is to admit that they have been allowed to appear as such.

To the man of prayer the haphazard events of life are not mere flotsam—he himself not some casual piece of wreckage drifting on the sea's surface and at the mercy of the waves— but to him the very ripples that sparkle in the sun, no less than the groundswells which move in courses too deep for him to follow, are so many evidences of God's love.

COROLLARY

TO claim that the only happy people in the world are those who have died to the world is to claim too much. What may be true of absolute happiness, need not be true of relative happiness.

Certainly there are worldly people who are happy. But perhaps not many. And perhaps not very happy—or perhaps gay rather than happy. And perhaps not for long.

For solid happiness you have to have a standard of comparison, you must be able to treat praise and blame with equanimity, you must not allow material possessions to fill your horizon, and you must be proof against the doctrines of a cheap philosophy.

The happiness of the worldling is, at best, like that of the child. The child thinks he is happy because he knows no better. The child takes his happiness as a matter of course, neither questioning his right to it nor analysing what it is. If the worldling enjoys his life in this way, assuming everything, he can presumably possess a happiness of a sort.

For as long as people think that their enjoyment of creatures is happiness, it is what they think. But they must have uncritical minds to be able to think like that at all.

Even the most pronounced hedonist will fail to maintain his

state of happiness for long if there is self-deception in his boast as to the sources of it.

So you get this curious paradox, that though it is in the interests of the world to promote self-deception, there is nothing like self-deception for ultimately producing disgust for the world. It is almost impossible to keep oneself genuinely deceived throughout one's life.

But it would be a mistake (and very wrong) for religious people to imagine that most worldly people, whether happy or unhappy, were the victims of one or other form of self-deception. There is just as much self-deception among religious people. Probably more.

If we want to know if it is a warm day, we should not ask the man who is sitting over a fire. If we want to know about happiness, real happiness, we should not ask the hedonist but the saint.

And the sad thing is that when we question the people who are trying to be saints we find some—not many, but a few—who are doubtful as to whether they are happy in either sense. If this doubt is not due to a natural melancholy, which should in any case be vigorously mortified, it means that something is being missed of what Christ came to bring and what religion is intended to develop.

It is hard to be happy if you expect to be unhappy. It means that you approach life with suspicion, with mental reservations, with ready bolt-holes which will secure your escape into unreality. The combination of suspicion and self-pity kills the chances of happiness stone dead. Happiness will not force itself down your throat.

It is equally hard to be happy if you expect your happiness to come from one direction and from one direction only. Whatever it is that you identify your happiness with—short of God Himself—it will almost certainly turn out to be something else. The great thing then is to switch from the dream to the reality. But mankind at large chooses rather to live on in a dream that has been woven by self than to pick up a reality that has been sent by God.

People prefer to be restless, lonely, bitter and miserable in their own way than happy in the way chosen for them by God. It is not even that they think their own way spells a reflex kind of happiness in which they can find rest. It is simply that they will not take on what someone else has decided is best for them. Someone else here being God.

Pride and obstinacy are far greater evils to such souls than the worldly satisfactions into which they think they can escape. Sooner or later the worldly satisfactions will be seen to provide no escape. But unless there has been a complete change of heart, pride and obstinacy remain.

Such souls crave for the good that is offered, but the false satisfaction of denying the craving is stronger than the craving itself. From the time of St Augustine to our own—and perhaps never clearer than in our own time, and from the pen of an American religious—all this has been pointed out. But people will still break their teeth on a stone which they can call their own rather than eat the bread prepared for them by their Father.

The bitterness which such people feel all day is recognized as such, and despised for what it is. And when they see it in other people they know the cause of it and the remedy. Nevertheless they love it more than its opposite which is held out to them.

If people must crucify themselves it is sad that they should choose to do so alone.

They do not want to force their crucifixion on others, but inevitably people suffer on their account. And this, instead of telling them something about love, only makes things worse.

St Peter was crucified head downwards out of humility and love. The people whom we are considering are crucified upside down out of pride and bitterness. Theirs is a real enough cross, and all the harder to bear because the one Person who could teach them about it is not given a hearing. He is not properly seen by such people, for they are the wrong way up.

They know that love is the whole answer to their problem but they restrict the meaning of love to their own terms. But unless love is seen in God's terms, in the terms of Love Itself, the thing shrivels to nothing.

These people desperately want to love and be loved, but they have locked their hearts and thrown away the key. They know where the key can still be found, but they are too proud to be seen looking for it. Too proud to look, even if nobody sees them. Too proud to open up, even if the key is brought to them and placed, out of charity, in the lock.

Charity is not dead in such souls—it would be less trouble to them, they feel, if it were—but it is in chains. The sight of charity in others makes them envious. But they do not admit this: they are not humble enough.

Humility is not dead in them either—because charity and humility go together, and if charity is alive humility must be too—but it is upside down. It treads on itself. It is a good thing to lower oneself out of love: it is a bad thing to stamp on oneself out of disgust.

Without humility a man can find out nothing about himself. Without humility he will dramatize and idealize himself until there is nothing of his real self left.

In fact without humility it is difficult to see how a man can even begin to be happy. If happiness comes of being the person you are meant to be, and doing the things you are meant to do, and thinking the things you are meant to think, humility is absolutely necessary as a foundation.

Your humility will insist that you do not dictate to God about your place in His universe. You will not be, and act, and think, independently of what He wants you to be, and do, and think. Your humility will insist that you conform.

So long as a man is trying to be what God wants him to be, even if he does not yet know what this is, he should be happy. He should be happy looking for God's will, and happier still when he learns what it is. It is not trying to know that keeps people from happiness. It is trying *not* to know that makes them positively unhappy. Then it is very hell.

But if his eagerness to discover God's plan for him is based solely on the happiness he expects to find in it, there is nothing to insure his success. He may well miss both God's plan and his own happiness.

It is not so difficult either to know or to be what God wants you to be, provided you do not want to be anything else. Once you have your own portrait of yourself as your desire, you leave no room for discovering, or being, your real self.

When the desire to be the self which you have designed outlasts the effort it costs you to arrive at that false self, then there is danger for you. It means that every day you are getting harder in a tyrannous mould.

Your impersonation has added nothing to you, and has taken away much. All you have done is to assemble together into an unreal person the separate qualities which you admire in others. If instead you were to take whatever real qualities you have got, and let them make up the person whom God has created, you would have something true at the end of it. This way you might not appear, either to yourself or to others, as much of a hero; but at least you would be true.

To live the part in your own imagination only is not to live at all. It is a borrowed life, and it is not even being borrowed from God who is the Author of Life. It is being borrowed from fiction. God does not bless what He has not created.

'Remember, man, that thou art dust, and unto dust thou shalt return.' Man is not made out of smoke, or from bubbles, or out of vibrations in the air that can be caught and projected on a screen. Dust may not be romantic, but there could be nothing more real.

There are implications to be found in this. If man had been fashioned from something that could evaporate, there would be nothing for him to return to. But a man, even while he is living in the flesh, can return to his constituent element: he does this the moment he is ready to be what God has made him.

If it is madness to project yourself into the part which God does not want you to play, it is hardly less foolish to impose this false self of yours upon your friends. How can they come to the rescue of a person whom they cannot get hold of?

41

If your one ambition is to qualify for the admiration of others, and if you show them a self which might be admirable in some but which is not present in you, you will not only fail to live up to the idea you have created in their minds but you will also be cutting yourself off from their understanding. And it is difficult to see how a man can live in this world without being understood.

So long as you are an imaginary figure—even though you win a name which will be remembered for centuries, and even if there are statues and relics of you in museums—you are a nobody. You have no substance.

This or that part to be played, if it is an affectation merely, can be easily renounced. Such superficialities are detachable, like clothes which are put on and off. It is when in the mind they become a life, a reality, that they are menacing the soul's peace and happiness.

To be haunted by the fear of not living up to the idea of oneself which one has created in the minds of others is worse than the fear of not giving satisfaction to oneself. One gets used to being a disappointment to oneself sooner than one gets used to being a disappointment to others.

But in either case the effort to be what one is not destroys true liberty, and is very exhausting. How can the soul feel free when there is always the dread of exposure ? The only hope of freedom is to proclaim one's independence of the phantom figure whom one has built up out of nothing and to plunge into the reality which is God's will.

Once one has broken with servitude to the imagination, one finds little difficulty in seeing one's true vocation as the fulfil-ment of God's actual will. One no longer tries to force God into proclaiming a possible will. One accepts His immediate will, and that is enough. Here at last is true liberty, true peace.

Our whole business, then, is to forget the picture of our-selves which we see reflected in the characters whom we admire. These others have their characters, we have ours. We should forget too the picture of ourselves which we would like others to admire in us. And lastly we should forget the picture of ourselves which we would have painted had we been God. In fact we should forget the picture of ourselves altogether, and concentrate on finding in ourselves the reality which is Christ.

The married man who looks wistfully at the religious vocation, the active religious who sees himself happier and holier as a contemplative, the contemplative who is forever dreaming about death: each of these is bowing down before a ghost and wasting a lot of time.

What is happening is this. The married man is inventing friends who will say, 'There is Brother X who is so spiritual'; the active religious is inventing friends who will say, 'He is a hermit you know'; and the contemplative is composing an obituary notice which will read, 'He will be missed by innumerable souls to whom in his lifetime he brought comfort and strength.' It is foolish to be chained to a ghost.

But throughout this disquisition we have been talking as though happiness were all important to us in this life. It is not. Only the will of God is all-important. Happiness is an indication, an expression, a by-product of the will of God.

Do not the words 'Seek ye first the kingdom of God, and all these things will be added' tell us that we may not make happiness our primary aim? And those other words, to which we are always returning, about dying in this life so as to make sure of eternal life—do they not tell us also that the sacrifice of one happiness is the way in to another?

Even those who are wise with human wisdom can see good as coming to birth only through sacrificing and being sacrificed. The ideas of love and sacrifice are so close as to be almost the same idea: love sacrificing itself for love, sacrifice becoming the seal and expression of love. In art, too, the idea of immolation is never far off: *Der Mensch*, says Goethe of the artist, *muss wieder ruinirt werden*. Man has to be ground down and made into a new bread. The highest activities of man have their foundations deep in sacrifice.

We are not expected, even if it were found possible to do, to eliminate the desire for happiness. But we are expected to subordinate it. Though the instinct to search after happiness is placed in us by God, there are times when the duty of searching after the will of God must be allowed to come first.

It would be hypocrisy to say, 'I have sacrificed my happiness: it no longer means anything to me: all I want now is the greater glory of God.' It would be more true, as well as more humble, to say, 'I want God's glory to come first, and though I would like to forget about what I get out of it, I know that my sacrifice will be rewarded.'

When St Peter, looking for reassurance, asked our Lord what reward the disciples would receive for having left all, he was given the answer. They would be rewarded all right. But the next words our Lord spoke after that were about persecution and the cross.

So it does not do to think too much about happiness: it is safer to work at the process by which it is earned.

To be preoccupied by the thought of happiness, to let it have the deciding voice in questions of conduct, is to lay the soul open to greed, envy, fear. Even someone else's happiness, if it becomes to me an all-absorbing interest, destroys my freedom. The happiness of others, no less than my own, must be kept in its place in relation to God.

Where happiness, my own or another's, gets out of place in relation to God it upsets the order of everything else. It is apt to get into the place which is reserved for God alone.

If I wish to be truly free I have to be independent of passion. And there is no more cramping passion than the passion for happiness.

The rightly ordered desire for happiness becomes hope. The wrongly ordered desire for happiness becomes an obsession.

'If any man hate not his own life also,' says our Lord in St Luke's Gospel 'he cannot be my disciple.' 'Hate' is the word used by our Lord: there is, on the negative side, no stronger word in the language.

So if I am prepared to love, I must also be prepared to hate. 'You must deaden then those passions which belong to earth …

44

you must be quit of the old self and the habits that went with it; you must be clothed in the new ... risen then with Christ, you must lift your thought above, where Christ now sits at the right hand of God. You must be heavenly-minded, not earthly-minded; you have undergone death, and your life is hidden away now with Christ in God. Christ is your life, and when he is made manifest you too will be made manifest in glory with him.'

Sacrifice is always bound to be the supreme test. The higher the destiny proposed, the greater the suffering in its attainment. The closer the union to which the soul is called, the more searching will be the self-sacrifice.

The peace offered by the risen Christ is the peace won by the crucified Christ. And those who most truly possess this peace arrive at it not by the heroism of which pain is the occasion, but by charity of which it is the expression. It is not triumphing over suffering that wins us the love of God: it is the love of God that lets us see the point of suffering.

FREEDOM, PEACE, AND HUMILITY

FREEDOM is not only being able to choose; it is being able to renounce choice. That is why to choose God's will, even though it may tie you down to doing what you do not want to do, is an exercise of the greatest liberty. It means that you are refusing to choose according to nature, and are deliberately choosing according to grace. What larger freedom could there be than this?

To lay yourself open to whatever God sends, and to know all the time that He may decide to impose a slavery upon you, is to act in the spirit of true liberty. It means then that you share the freedom of the children of God: you are giving to the Father the freedom of His own will.

When God sees that your soul is in earnest about this, when He knows that you are acting according to a settled plan and not out of emotion or impulse, He draws your will into His. This does not necessarily mean that you have been admitted to what the mystics speak of as transforming union, or even that you have been admitted to an extraordinary grace of any kind, but it does mean that you enjoy the freedom of the Father's house.

When we read our Lord's words in St John's Gospel: 'As long as you live on in me and my words live on in you, you will be able to make what requests you will, and have it answered', and again later on in the same discourse, 'You have only to make any request of the Father and He will grant it to you. Until now you have not been making any requests in my name; make them and they will be granted'—when we read this we sometimes wonder why our requests are often not granted. The reason is that if we were united to the Father's will, if our prayers were truly 'in Christ's name', they would be. God's own will cannot be denied by God, and when our wills are truly His our prayers will be His as well, and as such will not be refused.

To request the will of God in our prayers is to show ourselves at our best before Him and at our most free. And, which is far more important, it is the prayer which gives Him the greatest praise.

Thus it would be a mistake to think of the freedom of the human will as expressing itself only in its acts of choice, only in the occasions of its exercise. By embracing the will of God it expresses itself continuously. The free choice, implicit and only intermittently articulated, is in the life itself—in the life of union with the free will of God.

I can say therefore that for so long as there is anything in my life, whether it is a happiness I have invented for myself or a person I am attached to or an interest I am clinging to, that is so placed as to overshadow God's will I am incapable of being free.

God's will is the basis of human freedom. Since freedom implies absence of limitation, from what source can we derive it save from Him whose infinity is His liberty?

We have said much about happiness, but freedom and peace are more important than happiness because they are the condition of happiness. They also explain happiness in a way which happiness does not explain them. The only thing that fully explains freedom and peace is the love of God.

But, like happiness, freedom and peace are means only. To the soul seeking after God they are symbols, expressions, foretastes. They are desirable in themselves but they are not ends in themselves. That is to say that the soul has a right to secure liberty and peace. Has even a duty to secure them. But what the soul may not do is to think that, possessing them, there is nothing more that need be done.

And another thing the soul may not do is to enjoy them without reference to God and without gratitude. Freedom and peace are His gift or they are nothing.

Wrongly understood, peace and freedom, like happiness, can become a drug. Once these goods from God's hand become drugs, they are found to be as unsatisfying as drugs. Peace and freedom, thus enjoyed, wear off. So it is absurd not to keep reminding oneself that they come from God's hand.

Though to settle down in the gifts of God is to destroy them, to enjoy them with due acknowledgment when everything about you has been destroyed is to increase them. Thus you can be free and at peace when your environment is against you. Possessing your soul under adverse conditions is not a mere holding operation: it is a growth in grace. It is a widening of your freedom and a deepening of your peace.

Some of the satisfactions for which men crave are dependent upon physical provisions. The appetite for companionship demands people, the appetite for rest demands sleep, and so on. Even the appetite for knowledge demands the existence of subjects to study. But the appetite for peace and liberty can be met by drawing upon reserves which are purely interior. When the peace and liberty of a soul are being built up by grace, prayer, and the sacraments, there is no disturbance that need upset them.

Persecution has proved that there are some things that

cannot be wrested from human beings. But it requires a high standard of valuation on the part of the persecuted to see that they are not. For spiritual freedom and for the peace of Christ, the standard of valuation is a supernatural one.

The mistake is to think that the fullness of liberty is the freedom to do wrong when you want to. The liberty is just as great, if not greater, that lets you do right when you want to. Sin is the antithesis of freedom. Sin is slavery. To turn one's back on slavery is clearly the first step towards emancipation.

Nor is freedom the power to limit and define the extent of your service of God. It may involve doing this, but freedom is something more than the permission from God to pass discretionary judgments.

You can say freely 'I give to God the practice of fasting on Fridays, but I do not give to God the use of the discipline.' This is all right: we live in a free world. But this is not freedom's whole story. The essential fact about freedom is that it is part of the freedom of God, and that it draws its criteria from the mind of God. Its judgments are made in the light of grace and nothing else.

Incorporated into the life of Christ, given the freedom of the family, the adopted son enjoys the privileges of the heir. The greatest act of freedom which the son can perform is that of deliberately giving up his own will in order perfectly to fulfil his Father's. The son's own will is his own 'freedom', and this it is his prerogative to repudiate.

'I came not to do my own will but the will of him who sent me.' Christ despoiled Himself of the least vestige of personal human right, becoming obedient to death, even the death of the cross. The criterion was not to be looked for in 'my will'— even Christ's—but in 'thy will', the Father's.

'Father, if it be possible that this chalice pass from me'— and it was possible. But Christ chose not what was possible but what was willed. All things are possible to God, but the question is what things are willed by Him. To choose all that is willed by God is to be free in the fullest possible sense.

48

Possessed as a habit, liberty shows itself in a hundred different ways. The choice of one saint in preference to another, the decision to take up one enterprise instead of another, the advice given to follow this rather than that course of action: these are the outward effects of liberty. In all this the soul is helped by reason, intuition, practical good sense. But for true liberty of spirit, there has to be the gift of grace.

Though it is not always easy to distinguish between the impulses of nature and the impulses of grace, it is easy enough to distinguish between the effects that follow them.

If you examine yourself on pride and humility you will learn which is at the back of your action, nature or grace.

Thus it is not the operation of grace which prompts the soul to run ahead and give to God either what He does not want or what He wants but does not want *now*. It looks like the exercise of the soul's freedom, and it looks like generosity. But it is neither: it is pride.

To decide what God ought to want, and to give it to Him, is patronage. It is not giving at all, but taking. Which is always pride's way. It is taking credit, and this is the worst kind of taking.

Where there is the desire to take there is no true liberty and no true humility. The acquisitive disproves the free: greed and detachment are in an inverse ratio to one another. The self-giving which looks for more in return than it surrenders is not an oblation but an assumption. Humility makes no assumptions. Humility, even in the eyes of the world, is unassuming.

It is always stressed that love casts out fear. But then love casts out everything that is opposed to grace. Humility too casts out fear. The soul that is emptied of self, and in whom there is no deception, contains nothing on which fear can fasten. The nothingness of the humble man secures his immunity.

Humility is not the willingness to protest, either before God or before others or before yourself, your lowliness. Nor is it the rational attitude of any sensible man who knows that there are others in the world who have more to be proud of than he has. Nor is it a mental knack, a pious fixation. It is a grace: it is a virtue which lets you value things in their just proportion, and yourself in relation to them.

Founded on the knowledge that God is all, humility is the state you are in when truth has uncovered you. When the last evasion has been exposed, and when the light of God searches deep into your hollowness, you know beyond all shadow of doubt that you are nothing. If the sight of your shame sends you off to nurse a sense of listlessness and defeat, you have wasted the grace of true humility. If it begets confidence in God you have co-operated with it.

Freedom, peace, humility: three manifestations of the same spirit or virtue—namely trust.

DETACHMENT, CALM, AND TOLERANCE

JUST as freedom, peace, and humility hang together and reflect one another, so detachment, calm, and tolerance do the same. Like a unit emerging from a unit in a Chinese box, this second combination of qualities emerges from the first.

The interplay of qualities is manifest: if we are to maintain ourselves in a state of tranquillity, and if we are to eliminate personal prejudice, we have to be detached; if we are to be forgiving and helpful and understanding, we have to be calm; and so on. But it is detachment that forms the base for the rest.

For making sound judgments, let alone for praying and for producing sound work, detachment is necessary. A man whose affections absorb him makes poor judgments: his reason is fogged by the emotion of the moment. In the same way a man who is wrapped up in the pleasure of the theatre makes distracted prayers, and the man who is always wanting a different place to live in produces indifferent work.

It follows then that if he is to find the environment best suited to the service of God, a man must rise above people, worldliness, possessions and places. He will never be able to withdraw completely from these things, but he must rise above them. That is to say he must not, in his ascent to God, let them weigh him down. And they will weigh him down if he gives them half a chance.

Since the question of the affections will be dealt with in the next section, we can confine ourselves here to saying that of all external detachments the shedding of what are called particular friendships comes first on the list. If the possession of material objects can have a blunting effect upon one's spiritual sensibilities, the possession of another person's devotion can have the same effect to a much greater degree.

There is nothing intrinsic either to possessions or to people that should necessitate the weakening of a soul's spiritual life. Created things, whether human or not, are good. The enjoyment of created things is good. It is the desire to possess them for oneself, to use them for personal gratification and not for whatever excellence they contain in themselves, that is bad. It is when created good is looked at more for the appetite it serves than for the Creator whom it reflects that the trouble begins.

Friendship is good. Indeed it is one of the most excellent of goods. It would be folly to deny the value of what relates so closely to charity. It would be folly, unless following a very clear call and under exceptional circumstances, to renounce the good of friendship. 'Nothing can be compared to a faithful friend' says Ecclesiasticus, 'and a faithful friend is the medicine of life and immortality.' This kind of friendship gives no trouble to the soul. It is the over-affectionate kind that has to be renounced.

But it would be no good to arrive at detachment from sentimental or exclusive relationships if all the energy thus saved were expended on attachment to goods, position, health, and comfort. Detachment is like killing an octopus: there is always something else.

51

As a rule the spiritual man is more on his guard against riches and luxury than he is against position and good name. But ambition can carry a man farther from the immediate duty of serving God than luxury. Luxury makes a man soft, but ambition makes a man hard. It is easier for grace to stiffen what is soft than to make the ruthless gentle.

There are spiritual men who will defend their good name with passion. Yes, yes, it is something to which they have a right. But to be inordinately attached to one's rights is no better and no worse than to be inordinately attached to one's figure or one's free time or one's prayer or one's corner seat in the train.

In the same way health, if a man sets too much store by it, is a distraction from the service of God. Souls are to be found who so love poverty that they would not waste a stamp, but who so love health that they waste months in looking after it.

Of all attachments the most difficult to recognize as such, and consequently the most difficult to renounce, is the attachment to the goods of the spirit. The same principle applies as to the other detachments. Spiritual luxuries are no less harmful, if indulged in, than bodily ones. If an extra-mural affection is a hindrance to the man who has chosen to wall himself up for the love of God, even an intra-mural affection is—if it is indulged in and fostered at the sacrifice of the true love of God —a departure from the purpose. Disguised as affection for God, excessive interest in sensible devotion is nothing else than affection for self. There is all the difference between being holy and enjoying the sensation of being holy.

If sensible devotion is sent by God as a spur to the will, it is to be received with thanksgiving and followed up with good works. It is, in this case, a good. But like other goods, it can be excessively coveted.

So far as detachment goes, the excessive desire for consolations in prayer is on the same plane, then, as excessive desire for anything else. The question for detachment to decide is not what is desired but what is excessive. The value of the thing desired does not sanctify the excess with which it is desired.

Such is the muddleheadedness of man that he can even love sanctity to excess. The only thing he cannot love to excess is God.

Out of detachment comes, inevitably, calm. The soul in whom the desires are balanced, in whom the faculties are ordered according to the order of God, is bound to be both serene and soothing: personally at harmony, and having a reassuring, tranquillizing, effect on other people.

The man whose emotions are at rest in their proper object, namely God, has time to look about him. He is not flustered. Disappointment does not stampede him. And all this he can communicate to others. If fear can spread from one to another, so can calm.

In the strength of the saint there is—since it is the strength of Christ that is in him—something of the modesty of Christ. To modern ears the word 'modesty' has an odd sound about it, but it is a favourite term among the writers of the Middle Ages: its meaning combines gentleness, reserve, aloofness, humility. There must be a *modestas* about the follower of Christ, showing itself in the hundred ways by which one human being reveals himself to another.

Then finally there is tolerance. The man who is able to stand back from the scene and make a cool assessment of what he sees, the man whose practical judgment is unencumbered, can take one of two views of the world. If the retreat from which he surveys mankind is a false retreat, that is to say if his calm comes from nature and not from having ordered his soul according to God, he may take the cynical view and condemn the world. If on the other hand the peace which he enjoys is the peace which Christ has given him and which the world cannot give, he will warm towards the world and see that it is good.

Thus the man who is detached and calm is the man who can afford to be tolerant. Tolerant, not because he is too lazy to be anything else—which is the reason why so many tolerant people are tolerant—but because he is free enough from prejudice to be able to see mankind as God sees it.

The saint is tolerant for three reasons: because he knows

God, because he knows himself, and because he knows that sinners are only fools. It is the near-saint who is intolerant of sinners, judging them to be full of malice when they should be turning to God with all their hearts. It is the near-saint who is intolerant with himself, seeing his many failures and trusting in what he knows to be a weak character. It is the near-saint who is intolerant of the world which God has made.

The mature soul, the soul that has learned something of the way in which grace works, is never exasperated, or even greatly disappointed, by results. The life of faith has taught him that he knows next to nothing about the universe, about mankind, about himself. He knows that the Providence of God takes care of all these things. Viewing life impersonally, as the selfless soul must, he is no longer in an agony of doubt when God appears to act unreasonably; no longer in an agony of anxiety when sinners go on sinning; no longer in an agony of self-disparagement when he himself is found to be no use at all. So of course he is tolerant. He is now wise with a new wisdom. He thinks he knows nothing about the universe, about mankind, about himself. But he is just the one who does.

To some the idea of a man who is detached, calm, tolerant makes little appeal. 'These cold, distant, marble figures' they will say, 'are a spineless lot ... give us someone with spirit.' Or 'Tolerant people may be easier to get on with, but if you are an idealist you have got to fight.'

But the qualities which have here been grouped together are to be understood in their positive, not in their negative, sense. If you think of detachment as ending there, if you think of calmness as not being in a hurry, if you think of tolerance of leaving well alone and taking no risks, you miss the force of these disciplines.

The term 'negative virtue' is an empty one, for the virtue which cannot assert itself is no virtue. And in practice, on the showing of those who have in the fullest measure possessed these virtues, humility is often found to be as combative as tolerance is found to be uncompromising. There is nothing supine in yielding to the unrestricted way of grace, nothing of a shrugged-shoulder acquiescence about the recognition of God's Providence.

Through the whole Christian philosophy the emphasis is seen to be on *being* and *doing* and *resisting*: emptiness and ridding the soul of responsibility are of the East. Surrender to God in faith is one thing, and leaving things to fate is another. Detachment, calm, tolerance may be products equally of Eastern and Western religion. But where Christ is the pattern of men's virtue, the detachment, calm, and tolerance are not passive but active, not negations but acquisitions.

THE AFFECTIONS

YOU can renounce your affections till you are black in the face but you will still go on getting caught up in them. That is just the difficulty: you turn your back on all this kind of emotion, and no sooner have you set yourself facing the right way than it returns to you and is as active as ever.

The first thing to get right is the principle. If you are clear about what God wants and does not want, you may hope that with His grace you will be strong enough to co-operate in practice. Where people go wrong in this matter of the affections is where they give themselves the benefit of the doubt: the theory of it has never been clear to them. They have a right to the benefit not of a doubt but of a certainty.

It is not your loving that God is against—He wants you to love others even as He loves—but it is the pleasure which you expect to get from your loving that God is against. He would even approve of getting pleasure out of your love if human love were part of your vocation—as it would be in the vocation to matrimony—but assuming that you know yourself to be called to renounce human in favour of divine love, the whole pleasure of love is handed over to Him.

Thus it is the pleasure-bringing loves, the romances, that

must be treated ruthlessly: the capacity for love must be treated gently and with infinite respect.

But it will be precisely the pleasure-bringing loves that you will want to keep and handle gently. You would not mind so much if you were asked to get rid of relationships formed in charity.

The factors to be considered, then, are pleasure and proportion. The preponderance of the first and the lack of the second are between them bound to deflect from charity.

If you love God Himself for the pleasure it gives you to love Him, He is not greatly glorified. So what glory does He get from it when we love others for the pleasure of loving?

Love is pointless if there is nothing in it of God's glory. It would not be love at all. *Deus caritas est*, and He cannot be excluded from Himself. The emotion that does not have its roots in charity is an anomaly. At best it is an uneasy substitute, at worst a parody. That which is not for Him is against Him, and a love which is not a praise is an attack.

Here you object that the reasoning is unfair, and that only the lowest kind of love, which is not worthy of the name of love at all, is that which loves the pleasure alone and gives no thought to the person loved. 'In practice one does not love people in that way' you say, 'and one certainly does not love God like that.'

To love inordinately is to love self. It is to seek as the object of one's love not the other person, or the other person's happiness, but one's own gratification. In the relationship with God it is possible so to love the superficial delights of religion as to substitute pleasure for God: in relationships with human beings the same selfishness can blind one both to the best interests of the other person and to the purpose of God.

So long as your affection has in it the element of greed, self-glorification, possessiveness, it will fail both the person loved and God Himself. And since these elements are present in all inordinate attachments, no inordinate attachment may find a place in the life of one who is given over to the ways of the spirit.

There is no romantic affection that is not in the last analysis, and in some degree, a glorification of oneself. This and the desire to possess are of the essence of such an attachment. So long as you want to impose yourself, your ideas, your affection upon another, for just so long are you trying to bind that other person to you. You do not admit as much to yourself, and perhaps you do not realize what is happening, but you are in fact laying claim to the ownership of another's self, ideas, affection. You are virtually trying to remove someone from God's control to your own. You are appointing yourself master.

Possessiveness with regard to people is far worse than the mere predatory instinct which seeks to acquire money and material goods. The detachment which stops short at human affection is no detachment at all.

'But where the desire to possess is in abeyance, is not in evidence at all ... and where the person loved is holy, better than oneself in every way ... must one be detached even from this sort of affection? ... such a relationship promotes rather than hinders the service of God, so what harm can there be?'

There can be much self-deception in this. Admittedly such a situation is better safeguarded than most, and it is possible that certain benefits may be felt on either side. But so far as detachment goes it does not make your human affection less inordinate to be in love with a saint than with a sinner.

Whatever is seen out of perspective is seen wrong. To be inordinately attached is to see with your desire rather than with your eyes. You will canonize what you want canonized, you will condone what you want condoned. A man in this state is no judge as to what is helping him in the service of God and what is not. All that he can do in this state is to ensure that he is not blinded to the true vision of God.

If you get dust in your eye, it matters little if it is gold dust or coal dust. The point is you cannot see.

Even to allow your affection to exist in the heart, without ever declaring it, or manoeuvring towards its recognition and reciprocation, is to act against detachment.

57

'But what if you cannot get rid of it? What if you accept all that has been said above, and sincerely try to put it into practice ... and it is there just the same?' Then the only thing is to look upon it as you would look upon an illness: it is an unavoidable contingency from which you must try to recover as soon as possible.

And like an illness, even though you may not have brought it on yourself, the affection has, objectively considered, a delaying effect upon your service of God. Indirectly, like any other obstacle, it may prove to be a formative influence in your sanctification. But this is wholly God's affair: you may not count on it.

God has His own reasons for allowing the experiences which are suffered by His creatures. But this is no reason why, if they are experiences of the heart, His creatures should allow them. Still less reason why His creatures should idealize them.

To idealize an unavoidable emotion because it is unavoidable and not because it is ideal is as bad as to make a hero out of a scoundrel because you cannot otherwise explain him away. In other words, you are being blackmailed by your unwillingness to face the truth.

It is the unavoidable experiences of life, and the instincts which operate irrespective of the will, that are the most likely to cause trouble. More closely do they have to be watched than the others, not less. And whether we like it or not the affective faculty is there, in us, all the time. Where we cannot call in a policeman to arrest Eros, we have to be all the more careful to restrict his activity.

The critics of such a repressive policy will cite examples to show that there were saints who allowed deep human attachments in their lives. The critics will further point out that Christ Himself 'loved Martha and Mary and their brother Lazarus', and that from among the twelve He singled out St John for special affection. Do these precedents not justify a greater liberty than here laid down?

They would justify your liberty only if you could prove that your affection not only lay inside the frame of God's will as declared to you in the terms of your vocation but also that it was entirely subject to the control of grace. In which case it would not be an attachment in the ordinary sense at all, but an expression of charity.

The full service of God in the ways of the spirit forbids that you have two circles of interest, one His and one your own. Either God is the intended centre of your life or you are. So long as you are either bi-centred or self-centred, you cannot be God-centred.

A man should think of himself as standing in a circle of God's light as an actor stands under a beam of light falling from the roof to the stage. Outside the light which covers him, and in which he moves, is darkness. There are other beams, other circular pools of light, in which other actors stand and move. But this is not his (the first actor's) business. One actor's light is so much outside another actor's light as to constitute, for each one, darkness. The circles are apart: each actor has his area defined for him: that is his particular area of light. For one actor to step outside his circle, to get into a position on the stage where the light cannot fall, to hide behind something or to walk off altogether, is to forfeit his right to light ... is to be in darkness.

When God and not man takes the initiative, letting the circles overlap and placing people inside the beam of light, He so arranges it that what is revealed is not romantic affection but charity. But there must be no nonsense about this: it has to be God's doing.

God does not introduce people into your circle of light who will trip you up or make you forget your lines. If their presence has this effect it is your fault. Or possibly theirs. But you cannot put the blame on Him.

Where the circles of the saints overlapped there was charity and not sentiment. Martha, Mary, Lazarus, John were inside the circle of the Father's will, not outside it. To have Marthas, Marys, and Johns in your circle, you would need to know that you had Christ at its centre. If your whole desire was to be found in Christ, there would be no danger that these others

59

might prove rival centres. If Christ supplied your whole need you would not want them to.

Also it is idle to cite the affections of the saints unless you know something of the detachment of the saints. Still more, unless you know something of the charity of the saints. Often you cite them without knowing even their circumstances.

Also if your particular friends were to you what the saints' friends were to them, you would not be uneasy about them. If they were meant by God to be the furniture of your vocation, you would not worry about them on the score of detachment. Grace would see to that: you would *be* detached.

Where it is a question of receiving God's gifts, you do not worry: you accept them without wondering whether you ought to. You do not examine your conscience as to whether or not you are justified in enjoying good health, in being happy, in having found your vocation. The gifts that you have labelled gifts, when perhaps they are not gifts at all, are the ones that cause you misgiving.

No amount of gratitude will compensate for a pleasure which you are not intended by God to enjoy. Guarantees of good conduct are no more than a boast of your own strength of character. How can either such gratitude or such guarantees be blessed by God? They are the excuses of Saul who spared the flocks of Agag.

When the soul knows what sacrifices are demanded and cannot rise to them, it is better to admit weakness than to pile up other sacrifices in pretended ignorance. Ungenerosity confessed is better than generosity unwanted.

'But *do* I always know?' cries the puzzled soul. 'Is it not that I look back afterwards and *then* know? Why can I never know these things in time? You would think that there would be more warning signals than there are. Where there is no obvious sign, such as passion or recognizable temptation, how can I be expected to distinguish between what is inside my circle of light and what is not? How do I know when I am safely walking about in my own beam and when I am only imagining it?'

It should not need the evidence of passion or temptation to

tell you if you want to give and receive affection. Nor does a voice from heaven have to point out the difference between a heart that is divided and the heart that is single. The heart knows near enough.

And there are the external witnesses. How do you face your prayer? Is it, when such a relationship is going on in the background, the honest and open expression of your relationship with God? Is your work what it was, or has it gone stale? In your dealings with others, are you more glad to be with them or less? Is solitude irksome, silence a bore, and do you feel a stranger in your normal setting? Are you wondering what others would think—perhaps do think? How do you view the idea of separation (or if already separated, a re-union)? Have you planned the death-bed scene? What is your first thought when there is question of a change in your duties, in your time-table, in your future? Can you imagine at all what life would be like without this influence in it? Does jealousy play a part?

To answer such questions, and to draw your conclusions, you do not need a miracle of light. But you need the grace to be honest, and this is a grace to be prayed for.

It should be stressed that what has been said in this chapter relates not to what is sinful but to what, the proposed ideal being what it is, would be found to do harm. The aim, in treating the affections as we have done, is not to find a code of morality which is safe but a course of asceticism which is sanctifying.

If nothing is so sanctifying as to follow the right order of charity—which *is* sanctity—then no aspect of asceticism can be so important as to establish the right order of detachment.

It is not by instinct that we follow the right order of charity, but by training. This means that we need both the light to see and the strength to fulfil what we see. If the affections fell into place the moment we recognized them for what they are, there would be no difficulty. But the spiritual man, seeing them as reflexions of charity (which is what they are meant to be) and seeing them at the same time as being possible obstacles to

61

charity (which is what they can become), has need of clear-cut ascetical principles which he can translate into practice.

It would be hard to say which of the two mistakes is more common or more harmful: to trust to the vague hope that one's high ideals will carry one through, or to trust in having sanctions up one's sleeve which will insure the requisite measure of detachment. The truth is that one needs both.

A man must know that love is something which he serves, and not something that serves him.

Anything that a man goes to for enjoyment remains under the law of enjoyment. Anything that he gives to as an ideal remains to him an ideal, and gives back to him an ideal.

It is terrifying to think of the power which lies with the man who loves. He can, in the name of love, destroy love with love. If he does this, his love becomes not only lust but hate. But on the other hand he can, also in the name of love, make holy the love that is in him by nature.

Nor should the Christian soul find it so hard to make holy that which Christ has made holy in charity. The coat of Christ was designed in one piece. Man, not God, makes divisions in the cloth of love. But perhaps it is only the saints, and only the greatest among the saints, who do not cut pieces out of the seamless coat of Christ and who wear it as it is meant to be worn.

Union in Isolation

FROM the policy of allowing no play to the affections there arises, since the affections remain always alive, an intolerable loneliness of heart. The soul must expect this and allow for it. It is intolerable only as a human loneliness; it is tolerable when endured with the loneliness of Christ.

Debarred from the least expression of what you feel, debarred from so much as a look which would give away a secret which is between you and God alone, you are thrown back either upon yourself—whom by this time you know to be the most insufficient of all supports—or upon God.

By the terms of what you seriously believe to be your vocation you know yourself to be cut off, not only from the companionship which you particularly want, but also from all other human sympathies. You know that even were you to look to others for sympathy, you would find no comfort in it. You know that the vocation to the exclusive love of God demands as much. What perhaps you do not know, for God keeps the knowledge from you at the time, is that all this is the highest expression of human love. It is also the best possible preparation for the pure love of God. It is sacrifice.

Only that love which can make sacrifice of itself is love in the highest sense. Only that love which is worthy can endure the test of loneliness. Since it is loneliness that proves the love and the sacrifice, it is certainly going to be something which God will let you suffer. How else can He be assured that your desire to be with Him in His Passion is anything more than a pious wish? In letting you suffer it He lets you have the precedent of Gethsemani for your consolation. Your loneliness will not be like His, will not be occasioned by the same circumstances, will be hard to recognize as having any bearing upon the Passion. But it will be because of love that you are lonely, and it will be for you to do as He Himself did when His loneliness was such that He cried 'My God, my God, why hast thou forsaken me?'

Though the loneliness which has to do without creatures and the loneliness which has to do without the assurance of God are on different levels, they are, so far as the soul is concerned, one suffering: they are different sides of the same cross.

Your nature longs to live in one world, and your spirit longs to live in another. You feel that you could be happy living entirely for human love or entirely for divine love, but that one must always rob the other of satisfaction. You know that the two worlds are ideally only one world, but to you they are two.

And they are miles apart. And you know that you will never be at home in either.

Such is the struggle of conflicting attractions which goes on in some souls for as long as they live. It is bound to be a lonely struggle because the whole point of it is that they can get no relief from a victory to either side. The fact that there should be no question of one side winning or losing to the other—the fact there are no two sides to fight—is not understood. If it were understood there would be no loneliness. The loneliness is caused by the apparent necessity of having to do without the love of either God or man.

Thus you go on struggling to reconcile one with the other, convinced all the time that the very struggle is condemning you to love neither God nor man. Even though you may give a notional assent to the theory of love's essential unity, your actual interpretation denies it. Your experience of love, human and divine, runs so contrary to the doctrine laid down, and to the solution apparently found by the saints, that you despair. It is only when you submit to this, allowing your nervous exhaustion to dictate the policy of 'in that case the easiest thing is to love neither', that your charity towards God and man is seriously threatened.

Until this stage is reached, all is in the Providence of God and must be accepted as such in faith. You must believe that God has arranged for this struggle, for this loneliness, for this near-despair. It is the only way in which His purpose regarding you and your relationships could possibly be served.

Those whom you are fond of can be helped by you only in the degree that you continue to develop your vocation in Christ. Your words and letters will not help them: your suffering will. By sacrificing your relationships to God you are strengthening them in Christ. You are indirectly helping to strengthen the union of these other souls with God; you are directly strengthening the union of your own soul with God; and the relationships in which you are involved are by the very act of your sacrifice made stronger in charity and grace.

Christ was never more united to those whom He loved than when He was dying for them. He was never giving them more than when He was withdrawing from them to take His place at the Father's side. 'Greater love than this no man has, that he lay down his life for his friends.' How can it be right, asks the unbeliever, that the appointed Man of Destiny should throw away all chance of further influence? To us the answer is perfectly clear. But what is clear in the life and death of Christ is not so clear in the life and mystical death of human love.

Not until the soul is solitary, cut off by the sacrifice which seems to benefit neither God nor man, can the life of faith be truly proved. It is now that hope rescues the soul from despair, and that charity wins its triumphant but completely secret success. To the soul there is nothing to see but utter failure: human love has turned out to be either a delusion or a thing forbidden, divine love has escaped one altogether.

But to have known in one's loneliness such failure and to have acknowledged it is to have succeeded. It is not even as if man were expected to snatch victory *out of* defeat: all he has to do is to find Christ *in* it. And in doing so he finds himself as well as those whom he loves.

If solitude were a matter of finding a lonely place and keeping to it, there would be a number of solitaries even in this active age. Every generation produces its quota of men and women who like to be left alone. But solitude is a matter of being left spiritually alone, and people do not like that. So there are very few solitaries in the world.

In the spiritual kind of solitude you long for death but cannot die. You think that death alone can solve your problem and bring relief. You do not see yourself holding out indefinitely, and you feel that unless death comes soon you will go the whole length and commit the sin of despair. You long, but as second best to death, for a serious and painful illness which will take you, if only for a time, out of the turmoil. Cancer will at least, whatever else, numb your sensibility to the interior struggle, will call for all your effort to deal with sheer physical pain, will relieve you of the responsibility of trying to reconcile irreconcilable loves.

But what you do not see all this time is that God wants a different kind of death from you, and that you are already dying. The death you have been craving for is of your own choice, selfish, an escape. This disease that you have been hoping for has already come, but unlike the one you want it is healthy and life-giving. The growth that is in you is eating away the corrupt flesh: you are being healed.

God's mercy is such that, in the prayers that He receives from man, He distinguishes between the prayer-content that is towards Him and the prayer-content that is towards self. Having inspired man to pray for a certain good, He ignores man's mistaken interpretation of that good and answers the prayer by bringing about His own interpretation. But man, unseeing, still goes on wanting and praying for his own interpretation.

The solitude which God sends is not the solitude that the soul dreams about. The death that God sends is not the death that the soul wants. God's solutions seem to the soul to be no solutions whatever: they seem to increase the problem a hundredfold. But then the whole of the spiritual life is full of paradox. Seen in human terms the values are unintelligible, are inverted.

Only faith can explain the mystical truth that the deeper the soul penetrates into the mystical body the deeper will be the loneliness. On the face of it it sounds a contradiction. But it is what happens nevertheless. The vocation to live alone to God alone does not make for a sense of companionship. The fellowship of charity and of divine love is now a very secret thing; so secret that the soul may understand little of it while in this life, and may think that all is sorrow and waste and infidelity.

'You shall be made sorrowful but your sorrow shall be turned into joy. A woman when she is in labour has sorrow, because her hour is come. But when she has brought forth the child, she remembers no more the sorrow, for joy that a man is born into the world. So also you now indeed have sorrow. But I will see you again and your heart shall rejoice; and your joy no man shall take from you.'

Solitude is the prelude to union: loneliness is an apostolate of love. Those members of the mystical body who experience the solitude of being thus 'hidden in Christ' should know—though the knowledge will not feel very real to them—that they are bringing the highest good, namely love, to souls. Were they to mix their own human love with this love which comes from God they would weaken it. They would perhaps turn it into something different.

Love, then, is being conveyed throughout the mystical body by means of those cells which seem to be the most remote, the most isolated. But in fact they are not remote or isolated for they are being given to share in the loneliness of Christ's Passion. It is only through the merits of Christ's Passion that grace is able to circulate at all: the closer the soul comes to the Passion the more effective is its power to communicate love.

It is not for man to complain of his emptiness and loneliness: he is being privileged to reflect the emptiness of Christ. Nor is it for man to yearn for a different kind of life than that which God has given him—a life in which his failure as a servant of God might somehow be forgotten and compensated for in the comfort of human companionship—because it is in the struggle to achieve a harmony that his sanctity will consist. Man must realize that his hunger for the companionship of other men is a part of Christ's hunger for the return of men's love. The heart of Christ was human as well as divine, and it is not for the servant to be above his master. The mistake that the servant makes is to think only of his own conflicting loves when he should be thinking of his master's united love.

For the servant to imagine that by living a fuller life in Christ he will eliminate the call of human affection is no less a mistake than the other. There is no elimination of what Christ has redeemed. Purification, yes, and sanctification. But not destruction.

There is no short cut, and there is no partitioning of obligation. Love of its nature is a thing of mixed emotion and varied expression. Only in God is love simple. All that man can do is to model himself on Christ and to hope that out of what appears to be chaos, God is drawing order and obedience and fidelity. We 'bear about in our body the dying state of Jesus, so that the living power of Jesus may be manifested in our bodies too. Always we, alive as we are, are being given up to death for Jesus' sake, so that the living power of Jesus may be made manifest in this mortal nature of ours.' Significantly St Paul's next words to the Corinthians are, 'So death makes itself felt in us, and life in you.' St Paul, dead to self in the life of Christ, is the cell which imparts love and grace to the members of Christ's body. And St Paul, if anyone, knew loneliness.

THE CROSS

THE cross, as one would expect from its shape, means being pulled apart from opposite directions. It is not simply a straightforward matter of going from one known suffering to another until at the end of it one finds oneself resembling Christ. It is more a matter of not knowing in the least how to handle the suffering of the moment, of not in the least wanting to face the sufferings that are to come, and of not having the slightest idea that there is any likeness between one's own case and the cross of Christ.

In fact to the soul who is bent upon the perfect service of God this is the precise agony of suffering—the feeling that all is being wasted and that the sufferings of the Passion are being added to instead of relieved. So conscious is the soul of its own insufficiency, and shrinking, and self-pity, that to see all this in relation to Christ's suffering seems utter humbug. Better to keep quiet about likeness to Christ, and wait till one's dispositions are more generous. So the soul thinks, and it does no harm to think so: it is the corrective to pride. It would do harm only if the soul did in effect refuse to offer its sufferings in union with Christ's, did in effect keep quiet and wait for a more favourable occasion. But souls of prayer do not refuse: they go on offering. Every time they pray they renew their surrender, their self-dedication. It is just that they feel it to be useless and insincere. And this is quite beside the point.

If the test of prayer is not what we feel about prayer but whether we pray, then the test of suffering is not what we feel about suffering but whether we are willing to suffer. We shall not be asked about our presence of mind while suffering but about the direction of our will: if the will is set towards God while suffering, the suffering is incorporated into the Passion of Christ.

We are not expected to love suffering: we are expected to love Christ suffering. The value of the cross to us is not measured by what we see of it, but what we bear of it—with Christ. Perhaps our struggle prevents our seeing anything of it at all, *as* a cross, but if in the struggle we want God's will then the struggle itself is part of the cross of Christ.

Just as light from God received in prayer is not as a rule the sudden illumination that floods a problem and brings certainty, so neither is the cross something which must obviously be part of Christ's Passion. It is not a wooden shape with a hard edge that falls out of the skies; it is more often a weariness which comes up from one's heels and seems to spread over the whole body. By the time it has reached the mind it seems to have poisoned the system against further resistance in the struggle. But if it is the true cross, the resistance goes on nevertheless.

It is a pity that people are not told more about the particular kind of blindness and opposition which the cross arouses in the soul. What people are led to expect from themselves is often a sweet acquiescence and prayerful endurance. So that where these qualities are manifestly absent it is assumed that either the cross has not been Christ's cross or that the cross of Christ has been received and rejected.

The cross dictates its own terms. You may not say that this

or that aspect of it does not apply: there is a completeness about the cross which unintegrated man does not welcome. There is no part of man to which the cross may not penetrate, but because man is so many-sided, and has such a warren of escape-holes open to him, the cross has to follow him from one hiding-place to another, and this makes it all the harder for man to bear. The man who throws himself upon the mercy of God, giving himself to whatever crosses God may send, is far happier from the start. At least he does not carry the additional burden of running away.

Religious souls find that they can endure the nailing and the thirst. There are many who have prepared themselves for this all their lives. What causes them the most suffering, because for this they are seldom prepared, is the sense of not fitting the cross—and having to be stretched to a figure which they feel was never designed by God for man.

So long as you can still see the wood of the cross, knowing that it was on this kind of plank that Christ was crucified, you can find yourself rising to meet the challenge of love. But it is when the cross is out of sight behind you—and particularly when you are being pulled this way and that by human beings like yourself—that you begin to wonder if you are in the right place. You begin to look round for a Calvary that is somewhere else.

If you knew all along that the particular trial of the moment—or, which is worse because it is more lasting, this particular insufficiency of character—was the altar on which Christ wished to have you next to Him, you would not hesitate. Your weakness would be swallowed up in His strength. You would know that He would take the strain, would impart to you His generosity. You would know that the love which you were sharing at close quarters must compensate for everything. But of course the whole point is that you should not know—that you should do it because you believe.

Just as in worship or in charity there has to be faith, so in cross-bearing there has to be faith. How else can there be self-giving? Where Christ is felt to be only a few feet away, approving of all that we are doing for him, there may be consolation and gratitude. There can hardly be the fullness of faith.

On Calvary the two thieves were granted close proximity with Christ in their crucifixions. Does this mean, it might be asked, that they were not given the chance of making acts of perfect faith, and that Christ hung at their side only for their consolation? On the contrary, it was specifically in the matter of faith that they were being tested. But do not forget that the two men had not got the gospels before them: they lacked precedent. For us the case is different: we are with Thomas and must learn the truth that 'blessed are they that have not seen but have believed'. The two thieves had to see something before they could believe anything. With us it is the other way: we have to believe everything before we can see something.

The cross, like God Himself, is hidden in the cloud. The secrets of Calvary are revealed only in faith, and even then never more than obscurely. Man will always go on stumbling under his cross, fumbling his way in the darkness. It is another of the paradoxes of the spiritual life that the crosses which bring us nearest to Christ are those that seem to get most in the way.

Moreover the crosses which keep us from Christ's cross are those that we cling to as selfish possessions. These are not crosses at all, but superstitions. Man can attach himself to any created thing—even to a form of suffering. The burden which Christ invites us to bear with Him is His burden first, then ours. If He wants us to put it down, or to exchange it for another, He gains no glory from our continued carrying. There is no virtue in a purely personal cross-bearing which has no reference to Christ. There is only affectation, pride.

If the cross is carried as a symbol only, it can become an image like any other. Without the Crucified the cross is without honour. *With* the crucified, the cross has meaning and becomes sacred. Suffering as such has no virtue; suffering *with* the Man of Sorrows is the most sanctifying experience in the world.

71

If every suffering were immediately related to the cross of Christ, there would be no problem. But for one reason or another we allow suffering to separate us from the cross of Christ and the mystery of pain remains unsolved.

The real problem of suffering is not why people suffer, or which people suffer, or what the sufferings are that hurt most. The real problem is how to prevent people from misusing the sufferings that are sent to them.

To misinterpret the implication of suffering, to ignore the opportunity which suffering opens up, to grow hard under suffering: this is the supreme tragedy of pain.

The cross, again as its shape suggests, points either to salvation or condemnation, to love or to hate. Not only the cross but also the cross-bearer has the power either to heal or to afflict.

Rightly carried, the cross can make selfish men compassionate. Carried wrongly it can make kind men bitter. Certainly there are problems connected with the grace of suffering.

Never does a man need more light than when he is called upon to bear some uncommon cross. And never does he feel so completely in the dark. If he could accept his darkness as his cross, the cross itself would be far easier to bear.

Men talk about the philosophy of suffering, about the approach to suffering, about one or other way of lessening, or evading, or overriding, or even explaining away suffering. But you do not have to worry about any of this if you get love right. Love is the only thing that makes sense out of suffering.

THE MASS

AFTER dwelling upon the thought of the cross, we come to think how the principle of suffering with Christ can best be related to the principle of praying with Christ. The answer is to be found in the sacrifice of the Mass.

Though the Mass is not a continuation of Christ suffering it is nevertheless a continuation of Christ sacrificing. And since it is also a continuation of Christ's prayer it is the focus-point of Christian worship.

When the faithful bring their sacrifices and prayers to the altar at Mass they are performing the fullest act of adoration that is open to them. The intrinsic value of their prayers and sacrifices may be little, but once united with Christ's action their intrinsic value is forgotten. What goes up to God from man goes up in Christ's name.

At the sacrifice of the Old Law the Jews provided the material for sacrifice: the faithful had the satisfaction of making concrete contribution to the act which gave praise to God and brought atonement for sin. Under the New Law we no longer bring animals as victims, we bring ourselves.

You may say that it is easy enough to bring oneself as an offering to God when one knows very well that there is to be no knife or flame. You may say that it costs one less that way, when one does not even have to pay for a lamb. You may say that if sacrifice is of the essence of religion, then the Jews seem to show up in a better light than we.

Sacrifice *is* of the essence of religion, but the point here is that the infinitely meritorious sacrifice of Christ assimilates into itself the finite sacrifices offered by men; and that this being so, it matters little by what outward symbols, whether expensive or cheap, those sacrifices are represented.

The victims slain in the sacrifice of the Old Testament, which were mere figures, are replaced by the divine victim Christ. Christ in the Mass is not a symbol but a reality. The Mass is not a commemoration of the idea of Calvary; it is the bloodless renewal of Christ's death on Calvary. It is not the sacrifice of an image; it is the sacrifice of a Person.

Until we understand how the Mass is Christ's sacrifice *and* ours we understand the Mass incompletely: we see it as something to be witnessed instead of as something to be shared. The priest at the altar is not performing a rite on his own; the faithful are not privileged bystanders. The priest and the faithful are united in the same worship, and their combined

73

worship is united with the infinite and adequate worship which is offered by Christ to the Father.

So it follows that the more the faithful accustom themselves to taking part in the sequences of the Mass's action the more fruitful will be their Mass attendance. The more Mass-minded they become during the actual time of Mass the more they are likely to carry out the implications of the Mass during their out-of-Mass hours. Steeped in the prayers of the Mass, familiar with the symbolism of the Mass, alive to the varying inspiration expressed in the liturgy of the Mass, the soul will meet the circumstances of life with the mind of Christ.

Just as Christ in His lifetime was accessible to all, was at the mercy of human beings, was obedient to the unfolding of His Father's will, so the man who has learned the lessons of the Mass as they are meant to be learned will show the same readiness to be handled by people and by life. He will live his life upon the paten; his sufferings will be always in the chalice.

Where there might be a danger of subjectivism in solitary prayer, the prayer which is made while co-operating with the prayer of Christ at the Mass is inevitably objective: the whole bent of the soul is towards Christ, Priest and Victim, and away from self. Yielding to the attraction of Christ's sacrificial prayer, the soul is drawn away from the contemplation of self and the range of its vision is found to be illimitable.

In the Mass is doctrine, history, tradition, poetry, symbolism, mystery, beauty, mysticism. The soul that fails to find in all this a quarry for its prayer must be singularly lacking in either purpose or imagination. The material is there, and the direction is there, so all the soul has to do is to surrender to the impulse of grace. And certainly the impulse of grace is there.

Though the question is academic and of no importance, it is difficult to see how, without the Mass, the soul could get along at all. Not even the Divine Office can be thought of as standing on its own, independent of the Mass which it surrounds and to which it leads up and which is its climax. Certainly the Divine Office is not an alternative to the Mass, could never be a substitute for the Mass. The whole system of the liturgy—with its cycle of feasts and seasons, with its lessons and hymns appropriate to the day, with its background of psalms—is concentrated on the Mass in such a way that the various hours of the Divine Office are reverberating echoes of the missal.

The man who comes to know his missal—not merely knowing his way *about* the missal, but knowing how to make the Church's prayers his own—comes at the same time to know something of theology. The feasts for him are more than stimulants to devotion; they are studies in doctrine. Even leaving aside for the moment the element of grace—which is the main thing in the soul's relation to the Mass—the ground covered in the mere reading of the missal is enormous. Nothing combines the study of Scripture, theology, hagiology, and traditional custom so adequately as the compendium which is at the same time the official prayer-book of the Church.

All the same it would be the greatest mistake to think of the Mass as being the Church's way of putting to the faithful what might just as well be put to them from the pulpit or in the classroom. The Mass preaches and teaches incidentally: its essential act is that of worship by sacrifice.

Of the four ends for which the Mass is offered, that of worship is the most fundamental. But petition is the one with which the faithful are most familiar. Most of us assume that we come to Mass in order to praise God: we are perhaps more explicit in what we hope to obtain from Him. Most of us, particularly if we follow the Ordinary, make acts of gratitude and reparation: it is our particular intentions, however, that seem to manoeuvre themselves into the best positions.

Though the Church means us to bring our petitions to the altar of God—and to do so is in itself an act of homage to Him who is thereby acknowledged as being all-powerful—we should be careful to avoid turning the Mass into a spiritual machine for the granting of requests.

Where there is faith there is almost always the danger of superstition. We can become so convinced of the Mass's power that we can fix our attention upon what it can do for us and so forget what it does in itself. It is a common error to *use* the Mass for personal ends, instead of *offering* the Mass for the ends which the Church proposes. The prayers that we bring to the altar are prayers that belong to Christ, that are shared with the Communion of Saints, that are expressed, either implicitly or explicitly, by the priest. It would be a pity if, in the middle of this great communal act of worship, we hollowed out a space which was reserved for ourselves alone. And particularly would it be a pity if we made this the main object of our coming to Mass at all or the reason for the careful attention with which we follow it.

THE DIVINE OFFICE

SO far we have treated of prayer either as made in solitude or during Mass; the prayer now to be dealt with is the public prayer of the religious in choir. This prayer is not the whole of the liturgy but since it forms so large a part of it, the principles set out in the encyclical *Mediator Dei* may be taken to apply. From this authority we learn that the liturgy 'finds its fullest expression in contemplation'.

The Divine Office then is not a vocal prayer primarily but a contemplative prayer. Expressed verbally, it is prayed contemplatively. The words and sentiments and chants are there, but through them the interior life of the soul stretches out in worship to God. It is as if the pages of the breviary were transparent, and that the soul took the printed prayers with it on its way.

Those who imagine that their whole duty towards the Divine Office is fulfilled by the careful observance of the rubrics and the articulate enunciation of the syllables are remote from the main purpose. The main purpose is to join interiorly with Christ in paying homage to the Father.

The homage rendered in the recitation or chanting of the psalms is the homage offered by the whole mystical body,

Head and members. And because matter as well as spirit must pay its debt of praise, there must be outward forms to show that the physical is in harmony of worship with the spiritual.

But because it is always easier to cultivate the outward than the inward, the Martha side of the liturgy has a way of asserting itself at the sacrifice of the Mary side. At least when you are singing or reciting or performing the stipulated movements of the choir you are doing something. You have something which yields to measurement: you can tell, more or less, whether you are doing the thing properly or not.

It is the fear of not doing enough in prayer, as much as the desire to make a display in church, that leads to ritualism and 'vain repetition'.

Ritualism as such is not encouraged in the Church. It is an accident to the essential liturgy; it is what over elaboration is in art; it is decoration made flamboyant. The ceremonial of the Divine Office is not so much a drill imposed from without as a system of bodily gesture which emerges out of a given prayer-exercise.

Ceremonies, rightly conceived, are good manners while praying. They began as spontaneous acts of devotion, developed into suitable customs, and finally crystallized into rubrics to be observed by all who are bound to the Divine Office. There is nothing either particularly right or particularly wrong about this: it is the way that tradition becomes law. What it shows is that ceremonial can never be as important as the act to which it is attached—namely the prayer act.

Nor is the multiplication of words for the sake of multiplication encouraged by the Church. In the recurring psalmody, the same psalms and antiphons and chapters coming round week after week; it is not the mere repetition that is of value in the sight of God; what is of value is the disposition of soul which is content to go on repeating the familiar prayers without looking for the interest of novelty.

In his book *Perfection Chrétienne et Contemplation*, Père Garrigou-Lagrange refers to the liturgy as a means of preparing for contemplation. But surely it is more than this?

Is it not itself a form of contemplation—an exercise in which the contemplative act can be as fruitfully employed as when praying in solitude?

Where the intellect, will, memory and imagination are directed towards God, and where the outward senses are acting in conjunction with this inward elevation, you get a state of soul which could hardly be called anything else than contemplative. The whole man, with all his faculties recollected into unity, is at rest in the proper object of his desire. Certainly a soul can be contemplative in choir.

Thus in a sense the Divine Office is not so much a preparation as a culmination: it is the crowning of the interior endeavours which have been going on in private. The Divine Office does not guarantee contemplation where there is no contemplative prayer before, but it does provide a medium for contemplative prayer where contemplation is there already.

An objection is sometimes raised that the long hours spent by religious in choir might better be spent in work for souls. But the Divine Office *is* work for souls. The apostolate feeds upon what is generated, and again and again regenerated, in the choir. The Divine Office is the Church's indirect apologetic: its influence, if we make any allowance for the supernatural, penetrates more deeply behind the barriers of unbelief, ignorance, hostility, than anything that is done by more immediate contact. Allowing that grace is stronger than argument, and that the scope of the liturgy is not confined to the four walls between which it happens to be observed, the prayer of the choir can be counted as an essentially missionary activity.

With every *Dominus vobiscum* the believer and the unbeliever alike receive something from the prayer-life of the Church which he will not get out of a book. Every *Kyrie eleison* brings down upon him a mercy which he is either too busy, too ignorant, or too lazy to ask for. It is from the treasuries of the liturgy that man, whether he knows it or not, draws pardon and grace.

When the world again comes to recognize what it recognized in the ages of the Faith it will not be surprised to find that its inheritance has been preserved over the years of materialism and unbelief in the centres where the Divine Office has been faithfully prayed.

To conceive of the psalter being out of date, to imagine that the time has come for a revision of ideas about the liturgy as a worthwhile occupation for educated men and women, to plan a substitute which can be carried into the world as a spearhead, and in lay dress with popular appeal, is to miss the nature of prayer altogether. What more fruitful prayer can there be, either in regard to the soul who prays or to those who benefit by the soul's prayer, than that which continues the prayer of Christ, joins with the prayer of the blessed in heaven, and recalls the human powers to their fullest possible function as originally designed?

For the religious the Divine Office is at once the warehouse from which he refurnishes his interior mansions when the ordinary store has worn out, the platform from which he preaches the inspired word of God, and the element in which his soul finds its freest expression. He can go on piling up metaphors like this for ever, and will not exhaust the possibilities: the Divine Office should become his second, and better, nature.

'But I am far more recollected out of choir ... there is no devotion, but rather exasperation, in having neighbours who cannot follow the common practice ... it is often more a penance than a prayer.' *Amice, ad quid venisti*?[1] You have come that you may do the will of God. You have said 'Lord, teach us how to pray', and now that He has told you how He wants you to pray, you bring objections. And if it is a penance as well as a prayer, the value is doubled.

Whether the soul feels at home or not in the liturgy does not greatly signify. The worship which it gives is the public tribute of the Church, and people do not always feel at home in public. The sense of satisfaction is not, and never is in things religious, the criterion. The quality which God looks for above all others in our liturgical worship is the desire to surrender

---

[1] 'Friend, to what purpose have you come?'

ourselves unconditionally to the action of His Spirit. And that is why the Divine Office can truly be said to re-present contemplation.

The Blessed Sacrament

CATHOLIC tradition rightly considers the Holy Eucharist, the sacrament of love, to be the centre and foundation of the mystical life. There is no Christian life without eucharistic life, and to think of a spirituality that could be built up apart from the grace of the Blessed Sacrament is to think as an unbeliever.

Souls have been deluded about their union with God in prayer: there can be no delusion about union with God in Holy Communion.

Souls have expressed their love of God in terms of every sort of image: they have never advanced beyond the forms under which Love Itself is conveyed to the soul in Holy Communion.

Souls have received strength and inspiration from directors, books, sermons, art and nature: they have received infinitely more strength and inspiration from Holy Communion and have been far less aware of it.

Souls have looked for peace in a hundred different directions. If they made Christ in the Blessed Sacrament their whole and only peace, they would find it more surely than in anything else. And if this peace were denied them, they would find in Holy Communion the grace of being able to do without it.

'No place else is there to be found such copious grace as here' says Tauler in his *Institutions*, 'where the senses and faculties of the soul are recollected and united by the power and efficacy of the bodily presence of our Lord Jesus Christ.'

Earlier in this book we have stressed the need for detachment: there is nothing that detaches the soul more completely, and at the same time more smoothly and gently, than the sacrament of the Holy Eucharist. In a way which is so subtle that the soul has no idea of what is going on, frequent Holy Communion 'draws all things to itself', purifying the desires of the soul and increasing its appreciation of the interior life.

A mistake which the soul can make in this matter of the influence of frequent Holy Communion upon detachment and a love of spirituality is to imagine that the relationship between cause and effect is not only noticeable but immediate.

Though the grace of the sacrament is conveyed directly, bringing instantaneous strength to the soul, the supernaturalizing of the appetites is effected only by degrees. For the Holy Eucharist to bear full fruit, the soul has to respond to the particular impulse which is given to it by its frequent Communions, and this is a response which is proved only by the process of perseverance.

The dawn does not drive away the darkness in a single act; the spring does not follow the winter on a fixed day; the bud does not burst into flower while you watch it. The natural is a type of the supernatural, and though the work of grace is not pledged to reveal itself gradually, it more often brings about its effects by progressive than by dynamic change.

Souls, though they may make every effort in their preparations and thanksgivings, can become so used to frequent Communion (as they can get used to the repetitions in the cycle of nature) that they are inclined to underestimate the effects. This has nothing to do with routine Communions, where the communicant automatically moves up to the altar rails with the rest, but with the tendency to attribute whatever progress is made in the spiritual life not to the grace of the Holy Eucharist but to some other cause. Neither wise direction nor personal effort can possibly do the work of the Blessed Sacrament received in Holy Communion.

A man who has spent all his life in a windmill is likely to be puzzled when for the first time he sees an aeroplane preparing to take off: he will wonder where so strong a wind can come from that can turn the blades of the propeller at such a speed.

It will have to be explained to him that the power is from within. In the same way we tend to mistake the source of our spiritual activity.

We may learn a lot about God and about prayer and about holiness from observation—from without—but the real work is being done within, where grace is fashioning the soul in the image and likeness of Him who is received in Holy Communion.

Experience may act as a book of reference, extraordinary favours may come as confirmation of grace received, acts of zeal and even of heroic sanctity may be the expressions of a soul's love for God, but none of these things has the value of a single Holy Communion. It is Holy Communion that gives these things their value. The life of grace matters more than the life of acts, and it is only when they derive from the life of grace that acts have value in the sight of God. The main channel of grace to the soul is that of the Holy Eucharist.

Any saint will tell you that he would rather receive Holy Communion than anything else in the world. And if he is a saint who is not very theological he will add that the only thing he will miss when he gets to heaven is Holy Communion. All this is because he has love, and love is developed in him chiefly through the sacrament of the Holy Eucharist.

Any saint will tell you that he has no fear for the future of the universe and the human race because he knows that the sacramental presence of our Lord is with us till the end of the world, and that this means mercy. He knows it because he has hope, and hope is developed in him through the sacrament of the Holy Eucharist.

Any saint will tell you that the force of materialism is as nothing compared with the force of grace, and that since there is more power contained in a single consecrated Host than in the most destructive of atomic weapons we can do more for our fellow men by going to Communion for them than can be done against our fellow men by waging war. He will say this because he has faith, and faith is developed in him by the sacrament of the Holy Eucharist.

The saint is habitually aware, in a way in which the rest of us are only intermittently aware, that 'he who partakes of this bread will live for ever': he will be living in Christ and through Christ, even as Christ Himself lives in the Father. Understanding the implications of the indwelling of Christ, the saint, revivified each day in his sacramental union with God the Son and so with the Father and with the Holy Spirit, finds within himself the source of all good and the security against every evil. The Kingdom of God, which is the Kingdom of the Blessed Trinity, is given a new connotation. The soul's thanksgiving after Communion is a deepening of the realization of Christ's words 'the Kingdom of God is within you'.

We talk about Holy Communion being the remedy against temptation and the planting of virtue. This is indeed true but we must be careful not to mistake the process: the Holy Eucharist is not merely a medicine. To take Holy Communion as a cure for a tendency towards a certain sin might lead to a misconceived approach both to the sacrament itself and to the way in which grace operates on the soul. If you have a headache you take an aspirin, but if you have a weakness you must be built up until you are strong. Holy Communion does not exist primarily in order to take away a temptation or a sinful tendency: it exists primarily in order that the soul may be nourished and re-formed according to Christ.

When St Paul refers to his work of fashioning souls according to the pattern of Jesus Christ, of forming Him in them, he is giving us precisely the work which is done by the Holy Eucharist, and which he, indirectly and by letter, is trying to further. With every Communion the soul is restored in its likeness to God, and given strength to separate itself further from evil.

FROM considering the sacramental body of Christ we come naturally to consider the mystical body of Christ. As the consequence of being united to Christ in the Holy Eucharist, and in the measure that this union is deepened, we are the more closely united to one another.

Christ's human body, triumphing over death and now reigning in heaven, is complete and perfect. There can be no further growth to a body that enjoys the plenitude of good. But the body of His Church is still incomplete; it is in the process of development. The formation goes on throughout the centuries and throughout its members.

The Church is for ever growing towards maturity in Christ; and so also are its individual members. Only when 'we all meet into the unity of faith and of the knowledge of the Son of God, unto a perfect man, unto the measure of the age of the fullness of Christ' shall the Church reach its determined stature. And in the meantime each single member must go on being revivified by Christ's Spirit, living more and more as flesh of His flesh, mind of His mind, heart of His heart.

St Paul tells the Colossians that 'the body is Christ's' and that 'the head, from which the whole body by joints and bands being supplied with nourishment and compacted groweth unto the increase of God.' It is from Christ, the invisible head, that the members draw their vitality, and it is to the honour of the head, and to the purpose proposed in the mind of Christ, that the members are called to direct their activity.

If the members were not related to the head they would be useless to the body, and if all the members perished the head would cease to fulfil its purpose. Thus in the mystical body of Christ the members are necessary as the head is necessary. And because the head is perfect, the members must endeavour to correspond.

Nor is this relationship between head and members an imaginary or purely figurative one, as would be that between the founder of some human society and its members. If St

Paul can say that we are 'quickened in Christ', that we are 'built together into an habitation of God in the Spirit', that we are 'now the body of Christ and members of member', there must exist a true and living link. The head exercises a real and continuous influence, so that each member who serves the head is doing what Christ did when living on earth.

Commenting on the conversion of St Paul, St Augustine points out how the voice of God from heaven does not say 'Why do you persecute My saints?' but 'Why do you persecute Me?' That is, why do you persecute My members? The head stands for the members. And again: 'If the head went to such lengths, must not the members follow suit?'

So close is the bond which unites the faithful both to Christ and to one another that the works done in charity are His works, and are of value, therefore, to the whole community of the Church. Participating in His life, the faithful reproduce the works of Christ.

If the development of the individual contributes to the development of the whole, the development of the whole contributes to the development of the individual. Circulation in the body of Christ is interrupted only when the member refuses to perform its function, refuses to be controlled by the head.

Those who refuse to obey the Church are cutting themselves off from the life of Christ. Those who criticize the Church criticize Christ. Those who suffer for the Church suffer for Christ. Those who help one another in the Church are helping Christ.

In a healthy organism there is co-operation among members: no man ever hated his own flesh' we read in the Epistle to the Ephesians, 'but he nourishes it and cherishes it, as Christ also does the Church'. If someone aims a brick at your face, your arm goes up immediately to defend the more sensitive members. If your heart leaps for gladness, your eyes, mouth, and voice show at once that they share in the general joy.

Compassion and congratulation are significant expressions of membership in the mystical body. Where these qualities are neglected there is failure of responsibility: Christian life is essentially corporate life.

Unless the members are ready to contribute to one another's well-being directly, there is no guarantee that their desire to contribute indirectly will be honoured by God. It is true that by sanctifying oneself one helps others towards sanctity, but how can one sanctify oneself if one is not prepared to bring active help to other people?

The mystical body feeds upon charity, and charity is not an academic virtue. If the progress of the Church depends upon the collective effort of the faithful, it is a collective progress and not a collection of isolated efforts.

In order to serve the mystical body in true perfection the members must view their own sanctification in relation to other members, must see to it that their own functions within the body are in harmony with the functions of other organs. To ride roughshod over the path which a less active member is trying to follow is not only to trample on the sensibilities of a private individual but is to bruise the organism. Touch one cell and you touch them all throughout the body: bring health to one cell and every other cell is influenced for good.

It is a commonplace to point out the communicating quality of certain emotions. Enthusiasm, panic, restlessness, amusement—these things can pass from one to another instantaneously. If by nature we are made one in the human race, by grace we are made one in the mystical body. Within the mystical body a soul is able to spread either peace, love, trust, joy, recollection on the one hand, or else sin and unhappiness on the other.

So far we have considered only horizontal relationship within the body, and the common relationship of the member with the head. But there is also the vertical relationship: the subordination of subject to superior. Just as the human body is made up of parts which are not all equal in importance, so the mystical body supposes the same inequality and requires the same harmonious interaction.

The Church is not mystical and nothing else: it is an organi zation as well. Without a heirarchy of some sort, without a scaled authority handed down from master to disciple, the organism would be unbalanced. A body that was all head and chest might contain the noblest things, but it would be incomplete as a body. In several places St Paul has shown, and St Augustine after him has elaborated the idea, how the sacred gifts and functions are so distributed among the ministers of the Lord that all combine to form the perfect whole. All the various offices are informed by the same Holy Spirit and are correlated in charity.

From those members of the body who are called to govern, an account will be required which is different in kind and in degree from the response which is expected of those who are called to obey. The nearer the soul gets to the head, the closer should be the resemblance.

If each member is called to sacrifice itself for its proper function, the sacrifice of those that are specifically dedicated to the service of God must be very great indeed. If the reason for my existence is the service of divine love in the religious life, the quality of my sacrifice must bear a special resemblance to the Passion. It will be as a particularly sacrificing cell that I shall find my place in the mystical body.

Should I fail in my degree as a religious I forfeit my right to the manifold services which I receive at every moment of my life from the innumerable other members of the body. If I am not the cell that I am meant to be, or if I am making only a tithe of the contribution that I am meant to make, how dare I claim my sheltered place within the Church ? I owe a threefold obligation: upwards to my superiors in religion, horizontally to those who share my level, and downwards to those over whom I have been placed in authority. By neglecting any one of these responsibilities, and in the measure that I neglect it, I am renouncing a help which eventually I shall find that I cannot do without.

Our security is conditioned by our solidarity. Unless we lean upon one another, and offer ourselves to be leant on, we are no better than solitary reeds which pierce the hand.

The life of the Church, then, is the life of Christ re-lived in the Church's subjects. The history of the Church is simply the story of Christ reproducing His incarnation in the soul of every one of His faithful. The mystical body is the living organism to which each individual cell brings its service as service done to Christ. 'Jesus Christ yesterday, to-day, and the same for ever.'

CAELI FENESTRA

THOUGH the title Mother of the Mystical Body may be disliked by some—on the grounds that if Mary is herself a member of the mystical body she cannot at the same time be its mother—it is nevertheless a title which has fullest theological support. If Mary is mother of the body of Christ, she is mother of the whole body. Mother of the physical body, she cannot but be mother of the mystical body as well.

We have seen in the foregoing study that the mystical body is constantly tending towards the perfection of its stature in Christ. When humanity, which is all the time being built up in grace, stands ready to be reunited to God, then will the mystical body be exactly measured to the plenitude of perfection as originally conceived in the mind of God and as actually realized in the Person of Christ. When this happens there will be nothing more for the mystical body to do on earth, and it is the opinion of theologians that the end of the world will immediately follow.

Mary, mother of Christ and of humanity in Christ, is uninterruptedly working towards this final restoration of the race and union of all mankind with God. As Eve introduced estrangement and enmity into the world, so Mary introduces unity and peace. As Adam represented the human race, so Christ represents the human race: as Christ comes to restore peace, so Mary, mother of the mystical body, comes to restore the disposition for peace.

Since prophecy speaks of Mary as 'crushing the serpent's head', we can conclude that it will be by her act that the last remnants of evil will be destroyed, and that it is she who is destined to lead in the regenerated race before God. In its encounter with the first Eve the serpent was victorious, in its encounter with the second Eve it is for ever losing strength and must finally be ground under her heel.

St John Damascene, in his homily on the Annunciation, has no doubt as to the place of Mary in the work of man's redemption and in the final sanctification of the mystical body of the Church: 'Hail to thee through whom we are enrolled in the one, holy, catholic and apostolic Church ... through whom we are withdrawn from the gates of hell and lifted up to heaven.'

St Anselm is no less clear: 'By thy fruitfulness, blessed Lady, a sinful world is justified; a world that was lost is saved; a banished world is restored to its true home.'

If Mary is mother of the mystical body, she is mother of every single member of it. And if Mary's will perfectly conforms to the divine will she never ceases effectively to desire for us what the head desires for its members.

As she was united with her Son on earth, perfectly co-operating with His sacrifice of Himself for man's redemption, so she is equally united with her Son in heaven and is equally co-operating in the redemptive work of grace among living souls on earth.

When we speak of Mary as being *our* mother as well as our Lord's, we are not merely stretching the word for devotional use. The relationship, though spiritual, is real. Through Mary we are begotten to the life of the spirit. We owe it to her, after God, that we are born to grace. As children of God we possess a supernatural life which could not have come to us but for her, and we must believe that, if motherhood has any meaning, her influence in the preservation and development of that life continues.

Though her sinlessness puts Mary in a position not shared by fallen man, her freedom of response to grace is the same freedom which the rest of us enjoy. The difference lies, not in the manner by which she responds, but the degree to which she responds.

It is only falsehood in one or other of its many forms that is the obstacle to the soul's response to grace. Where there is the disposition of truth, the infusion of truth can be effected immediately. Since Mary's soul was entirely true from the first instant of its conception there was never anything which could for one split second delay or hamper the direct action of grace. She accordingly becomes the perfectly free channel of grace to others.

The reason why certain souls are said to be saints is that they are judged to be established in truth and charity. Sanctity is simply the result of infused grace received by the co-operating soul whereby the gifts of the Holy Spirit are developed to such an extent that the soul comes to live the full life of love.

Thus in the degree that the soul is without falsehood the life of charity is accelerated. 'The path of the just' we read in the Book of Proverbs, 'as a shining light goes forwards and increases even to perfect day'.

In the case of our Lady, who possessed the balance of soul possessed by our first parents before the Fall, the progress of charity during the time of her life on earth was continuous and accumulative. 'The initial plenitude of grace,' says Père Garrigou-Lagrange, 'which she had received from the moment of her immaculate conception, was multiplied by every act of charity, each one more intense than the preceding, and increasingly multiplied according to a marvellous progression which we could never calculate.'

The same authority goes on to show, by comparing the reaction of the soul to grace with the gravitational attraction of natural objects towards their centre, that souls in their approach to God are found to move with increasing momentum as they come nearer to divine union.

Becoming more and more selfless in its progress of charity, the soul, ever better reflecting the absolute selflessness of Mary, is able to render deeper and deeper service to others. Whatever their outward opportunity, and even if this outward opportunity is reduced to nothing at all, the saints, because they are the emptiest channels, are the most effective conductors of grace.

It was revealed to St Alphonsus that among his many works it was his labours among the perfect that pleased God most. 'It is only by the perfect,' he was told, 'that I am communicated from men to men.'

It is not only the sinners that oppose the spread of grace: it is those who should be perfect and are not. A want of simplicity, the dramatizing of a cross, the discordant note struck by any sort of false virtue: these are the things that militate against our likeness to Mary.

Lasst mir doch meine Träume[1] is our plaintive song when we find ourselves being drawn to the emptiness of perfect surrender. The soul of our Lady was not clouded by so much as a dream. *Ecce ancilla Domini; fiat mihi secundum verbum Tuum.*

So perfectly was Mary's soul in harmony with the divine will that there could be no vibrations that were not of the note of God, no virtues that were not entirely of the pattern, no love that could counterfeit the charity of Love itself. In such a soul could there be anything else but perfect contemplation?

Sometimes we think of the contemplative as cherishing the grace of his prayer as a private possession. But if we think of him so, as lost to the need of others, we think of him wrongly. Rather we should see him as a shadow of our Lady whose contemplation goes out from her soul over the whole world.

It is only because we have so many images and phantasms that infused contemplation cannot filter through. It is not that our Lady, when she 'pondered all these things in her heart', had different things than we have to ponder: it is simply that she pondered without prejudice, either inherited or devised.

[1] 'Leave me my dreams at least.'

IT is not enough to lay claim to a faith so vivid that it takes everything for granted and bothers about none of the reasons for its conviction.

It is not enough to love God so much that you need not trouble to think.

It is true that on more than one occasion our Lord said, 'Thy faith hath made thee whole', adding nothing about the necessity of studying the grounds of that faith. It is true that He said of the Magdalen 'Her sins are forgiven her because she loved much', adding nothing about the necessity of analysing either the nature or the object of her love. But the faith that makes whole cannot be possessed on no knowledge at all. You cannot love much unless you know something.

Allowing that theological study, like liturgical observance, can all too easily become an end in itself—man being prone to get himself so absorbed in the science as to forget what the science is for—there is nevertheless an obligation to know one's faith as well as to practise it, to have foundations of one's love and not merely the feeling of it.

What happens when holy emotions play one false? What happens when faith no longer burns and love begins to cool? If there is no intellectual groundwork to fall back upon—a solid hearthstone which retains the heat and on which new fires can be banked up—the soul is left without security.

Unless reason can come to the rescue when the emotions have exhausted themselves, the will has to do the work of feelings and faith. Ordinarily this is too much for the will. The will can carry its load only when it has the intellect to back it up.

Theology is not an extra. Theological formation of some sort, even if it is only (and for those whose state does not require of them something more) a thorough knowledge of the catechism, is a necessity.

Nor is theology something which may be necessary enough in cases of emergency—when there is a heresy to confute or an unbeliever to convert—but is something which is meant to give backbone to the everyday life of the Christian. Rightly used, the science of God and the things of God encourages the life of prayer as inevitably as it must give point to moral, social, and intellectual life.

Without a theology of some sort, how can a man find sanctions for his decisions, standards for his conduct, material for his prayer, purpose for his effort? At least a smattering of Christian knowledge is necessary for any kind of Christian life and if a soul aspires to the full Christian life of sanctity and contemplation the more knowledge possessed the better.

Theology is not primarily a help to the brain but to the soul. Wisdom, the highest of the Holy Spirit's gifts, is a flowering of knowledge. And knowledge is supported by the findings of theology.

Just as we should not act without thinking so we should not serve God without thinking. And since the service of God is man's highest act, it is the one which calls for the highest thought of which we are capable. Theology does not exist to do our thinking for us.

Theology exists to make our service both more reasonable and more fruitful. We need to know the nature both of authentic service and of the Authority whom we serve. The fact that we serve an infinite God is no reason why we should not bring to that service a very finite mind. The finite mind must carry us as far towards the infinite mind of God as it will go.

But in all this we must not mistake theology, which rests on divine revelation, for theodicy, which examines the nature of God by the sole light of reason. The one is a work of grace, deducing conclusions from what faith has revealed about truth; the other is a speculative philosophy.

There can be no orthodoxy, whether of faith or morals, without dogma. The dislike which orthodox and well-intentioned Christian souls sometimes feel towards theology may be caused by the distinction which is made between dogmatic and moral theology, and more especially to the hairsplitting which is common to both.

St Thomas sees sacred doctrine not as two authorities, two

revelations, two sciences, but as one. If dogmatic theology has divine mysteries as its primary object, and if moral theology has human acts, the study of these things—since God is the subject and the source—is properly one. According to St Thomas a system which includes the teaching of Scripture, revealed mysteries, sacraments, precepts and counsels, virtues, gifts of the Holy Ghost and the doctrine of grace, is one which contains so many features which overlap that it must be thought of as a whole.

But these academic questions can be left to the experts. What matters for us is that in its manifold expression, theology—whether dogmatic, moral, ascetic, or mystical in form—is a system capable of leading souls to the heights of perfection, and that as such it may not be scorned.

The man who is content to rub along without understanding why he rubs along is like a man who takes exercise without seeing the need for keeping healthy. He will not keep it up.

The man who claims to be able to believe, pray, control his passions without having a basis to his religion which he can account for is like a man who throws himself into the river without having learned to swim. Faith does not take the place of the laws of God—still less contradicts them—any more than it takes the place of the laws of nature, or contradicts them.

When the student of his faith complains humbly that he is ill equipped intellectually to master the subtleties of theology and that therefore he can practise blind submission and give himself to other things, he is not in fact being humble so much as inaccurate. Man, the rational animal, is endowed with certain powers which have an affinity with the powers possessed by God. An obligation rests upon man to operate these higher powers of his—and operate them moreover, if he aims at the heights, to their highest extent.

It is not more humble, but less, to operate only the lower faculties of man. The man of proved intellect who says 'I am good for nothing but feeding chickens and washing up' is not being humble. He is probably being funny or being vain. Certainly he is being inaccurate.

Just because a man may be possessed of many lowly gifts and few exalted ones, he may not play one lot off against another. All gifts come from God. In the Providence of God our gifts are proportioned to our needs, and it is for us to find the appropriate channel of correspondence between them. We do not give mystical theology to the children—any more than we give aspirins to them when they are hungry—but we do give them the catechism.

If it is our whole purpose in life to unite ourselves with God and His will, we have to submit to being shown the way. Books of devotion may show us some of the way, but we need books of explanation as well. We have to be taught how to come to terms with His law, how to dispose our minds towards His mysteries, how to order the gifts of nature and grace which are implanted in us.

Psychology may take us some of the way, but here again, as in the case of cosmology or natural ethics or any of the physical sciences, the mystical element is left out and there is no guarantee that revelation is authoritatively interpreted. There is a wealth of explanation in psychology, but since its particular province is the natural powers of the soul it can never do service for the science which has for its field not only the nature of God Himself and of His revealed truth but also the higher powers of the human soul and all that touches the phenomena of faith. No science save theology teaches precisely this.

'But even theology has its limitations,' you will say, 'and since it is evidently unable to give me satisfaction on all the questions that vex my soul, I feel free to look for my own answers and evolve an empirical system which will suit my particular enquiry.' Truth is the object of theology, but not all truth has been revealed to man. And even some of the truth that has been revealed is given to man in the form of mystery.

If there were no mystery there would be no faith. And if there were no faith there would be no theology. It is theology that makes sure the act of faith.

Though the act of faith is meant to be a leap in the dark, there is no virtue in not seeing as much as we can while we are leaping. Theology exists so as to cure us of unnecessary night-blindness.

SORROW AND JOY

WE do not need to be told so often that sorrow is the lot of man. We can pick up that knowledge by ourselves. But we do need to be told that joy is the lot of man. Because of this we are apt, after a certain stage, to forget. Man is meant to take both lots in his stride: he is not meant to fix his mind unduly upon either. He is to fix his mind on God from whom they come.

To make a cult of either sorrow or joy is madness. The cult of sorrow is no more morbid than the cult of pleasure: they both lead to misery and selfishness. Rightly organized, it might be a good thing to make a cult of other people's pleasure—just as, rightly organized, the attention to other people's sorrows becomes compassion—but it does not do to focus attention upon one's own. An act of gratitude for the one, and an act of submission to the other, and the soul passes on to other things. Nothing is so introverting as the tendency to pin down one's sorrows and joys.

It would be better to make a fetish of indifference—because at least nobody would take you seriously—than to make a fetish of either sorrow or joy. But it would be better still not to make a fetish of anything.

Earlier in this book we have suggested that success is more difficult to handle than failure. The reason for this is that we have less capacity for joy than we have for sorrow. The saturation point for earthly joy is sooner reached than the saturation point for suffering. Even the most convinced follower of pleasure will tell you that enjoyment, unless you are prepared to effect certain controls, very soon becomes insipid. Sorrow on the other hand seems to enlarge the capacity for suffering.

So although joy and sorrow are two sides of the same coin—sorrow being a wrecked joy, joy being a sorrow the right way up—you get this difference in the way that they operate: while it takes grace to make the soul find joy in sorrow, it takes only time, and not much time at that, to make the soul find sorrow in joy.

Our Lord has said that our sorrow may be turned into joy. He has also said that one reason for His coming is that we may have joy and that our joy may be full. The implication is that sorrow is not meant to last, but that joy is. Now this seems to reverse the conclusion which has been reached above. What, if any, is the explanation?

The explanation is simply that the joy held out to us by God is not the joy that reaches a certain point and then palls. It is a quite different joy, and one compatible with sorrow. This kind of joy we never get tired of, because it is a foretaste of the joy of heaven. This kind of joy outlasts all sorrows, compensates for all sorrows, reflects the joy of the risen Christ who triumphed over the sorrows of His Passion.

This kind of joy, since it comes with the peace of Christ, no man can take from us. Only our own sin can take it from us, only that criminal folly of ours which reverses the order of nature and grace, turning joy into sorrow and bitterness and hate. The sorrow that comes now is not the sorrow in which joy may be found.

So it is that there are two kinds of joy and two kinds of sorrow. By the mercy of God the wrong kind can be turned into the right: by the alchemy of love the passions are turned into beatitudes: by the mystery of the Resurrection the mystery of Good Friday is explained.

'Nevertheless' cries out the soul in its suffering, 'there is no joy in what I am now experiencing. I try to offer to God these trials that come to me, and they only get worse. I would not mind so much if I knew that He was being served by it all, but I go on giving Him these things and there is nothing to show that I am getting any nearer to heaven or that God is in any way glorified.'

Souls who are allowed by God to feel this dissatisfaction are normally granted at the same time to feel that the answer, if they could only apply it, lies in faith. And they are right. They must not look for recognition of their sacrifice, nor even too closely at the sacrifice itself: they must look in faith at Him to whom the sacrifice is offered.

Rather than say 'Lord, I am giving You this ... Lord, I am giving You that', they should say, 'I do not seem to be giving properly, Lord, so come and take.' Often souls make the mistake of looking at the hands that are giving instead of at the hands that are receiving. If souls looked more at Christ and less at their own dispositions, they would not be so tortured by what their sacrifice was costing them.

The less we think about how we are giving the better, and about what great things we are giving up. The self-forgetting sacrifice is more pleasing in the sight of God than the sacrifice which is full of self-torture.

God is better served by giving than by giving up. Better even than by giving is the service which the soul renders when allowing God perfect freedom to take. The reward to the soul is that God in fact does take—taking more than the soul knows to be there.

Neither the sorrows that we offer to God, then, nor the joys that we thank Him for, can ever amount to as much as the work which He can do in the soul if we only let Him have a free hand. Sorrows and joys are indeed made holy by being directed towards God, but when we make over ourselves to God it is not only what we feel that is being made holy, but what we are.

There are souls without number who would willingly sacrifice what they have and what they enjoy and what they want. They make the offering every day in their prayers. There are not so many who would sacrifice to God what they feel themselves to be. It is perhaps only by means of the grace of suffering that they come to make this final offering. Or else by the grace of true supernatural joy.

So it is faith and love, then, that give value to sorrow and joy. Without the supernatural purpose, sorrow is at best only ennobling and joy encouraging. Once given its direction towards God, sorrow becomes the mother of many virtues and joy becomes the disposition for their exercise. It is terrible to think that so much depends upon how we suffer our sorrows and enjoy our joys. The whole structure of our spirituality depends upon just that: whether with Christ or no.

THE CONTINUATION OF THE GOSPEL

SEEING Christ's Passion reproduced in our own sorrows is only one way of paying homage to His death. Another and a better way—better because less self-regarding—is to see His Passion reproduced in the world and in other people. Even in the world which knows nothing of Christ's Passion, and among people who do not understand their own misery.

The Passion is still going on, and people are not paying attention. Even those who profess Christianity are very vague about Christ's contemporary Passion. Wherever Christ's members are being persecuted, Christ's body is being crucified. Wherever there is mass hatred there is Calvary: love is being killed all over again.

Do even we, the followers, fully realize that Christ is still talking, and that the Sermon on the Mount is not finished? Do we realize that the gospel is a living history and that we are part of it? The events of Holy Week go on till the end of the world, and mankind will always be divided into two groups on account of it.

Christ is the first and the last, the alpha and the omega. It is Christ yesterday, to-day and the same for ever. We visit in prison not His *descendants*, but *Him;* we feed and clothe and shelter *Him.* The least of these little ones which we see every day is Christ.

The Passion of to-day is not an historical review, reminding us of what happened years ago: it is actual and present. We do not witness it from a distance as we would watch a pageant: we are in it. The gospel script is meant for three dimensional reproduction: it is going on all round us. We are surrounded by a humanity which has the hands and feet and side of Christ. And all we do is to look wistfully over the shoulders of His mystical body in the hopes of catching sight of the body He lived in nearly two thousand years ago. As always we are preferring our imagined picture to the existing and immediate reality.

Men and women who know much about the sacramental body of Christ in the Holy Eucharist, much about the historical body of Christ from biblical study, concern themselves hardly at all about the body that is suffering in cities, factories, prisons, pleasure centres and unjust business concerns.

The Sermon on the Mount receives from the world as little attention as the Passion. The voice of Christ goes on echoing down the centuries, and man goes on calculating upon how much discount he can reasonably allow himself on what he hears. The word of God is not like the word on a page: it is a living sound with vibrations that never stop ringing.

If you wonder why the voice of Christ speaking in the modern world is so imperfectly heard, you have only to look into your own conscience and ask yourself what you do on the occasions when you hear it.

No communication can be clearly received where the reception is partial and selective. Where whole areas of the soul are insulated, the force of the communication is lost. Even where the import of the gospel reaches an area which is receptive it is imperfectly understood: the context is lacking.

It is a scholastic axiom that whatever is received is received according to the dispositions of the recipient. If a man looks at the world through the key-hole of his front door, the beauty of God's creation is measured by the size of the lock. Only those who are leading the life of Christ can fully understand the meaning of Christ. To those who pick and choose among the words of Christ the gospel of Christ provides no full solution.

Throughout the Christian centuries men have experimented

with the gospel instead of accepting it whole. Some of its moral lessons have been applied to some of the world's moral disorders. There is no guarantee in the gospel that this will produce results, and in fact the remedies have not been so very successful. Christians to-day are not so outstandingly different from others as to excite wonder. They would be if the gospel had been given a chance, if the Christ-life had been lived, if love were made the basis of human relationship.

'Yes,' you will say, 'but the world sees only what it has the light to see, and it does not see the point of the Sermon on the Mount.' Whose fault is that? Not God's fault for not sending enough light. Has the world—has even the Christian world— ever tried to see the point of the Sermon on the Mount? Has it ever practised it?

For so long as men say that to forgive one's enemies is un-practical, to trust one another in business does not work, to look upon wealth as being merely lent to you and to be used for others as much as for yourself is madness, to avoid all occasions of sin is impossible—for as long as this is the view, these things *are* unpractical, unworkable, madness, impossible.

How can men trust one another if they do not agree on trusting God? How can they insist on human justice if they do not believe in divine justice? How can they even begin to love one another if they do not derive their ideas about love from Love itself?

The world's external problems cannot be solved by an external Christianity. Until nations and individuals have bound themselves to the Christian gospel as an interior principle, there is not the slightest hope that the Christian code will solve anything. Only on its own terms does it profess to save, and Christianity does not profess to be an external code.

Why is it that men who would not dream of interpreting Christ's words at the Last Supper gladly interpret them in the Sermon on the Mount? Why is it that among Catholics who fully believe the texts which have to do with the primacy of Peter there is what amounts to unbelief with regard to the texts about riches, marriage, and scandal?

If the doctrines of the gospel held good in the time of our Lord, they hold good still. It is idle to quote altered social conditions, a new mentality, different economic standards, rival claimants to truth. It is not that everything has changed; it is that everyone has compromised.

The people who read the gospel but do not see the gospel in the context of their own lives are like the Roman soldiers who watched the Crucifixion but did not see it as having the slightest relation to them.

We can look at Christ and not see Him. We can hear Him and not listen. We can build up an academic religion which is no more than a hollowed out tomb.

It may perhaps be wondered what all this has to do with the interior life. Why now a digression about a pagan and materialist world? Has not the contemplative enough to worry about as it is, caring for his own rather uncertain contemplation, without having to dwell upon the shortcomings of a section of mankind to which he does not belong?

The reason for dragging the world on to the contemplative horizon is the theme itself: namely that God's order must be seen as a whole if it is to be seen truly, and that the contemplative may not ignore any section of humanity's need. There is no part of humanity to which the contemplative does not belong. The whole point of what we have been considering is that the body of Christ is everywhere.

The contemplative, more than any, must see the world not only in unity, not only in the dimension of the spirit, not only as the object of God's continued love—'God so loved the world as to send His only-begotten Son'—but as an entity that is crying out for the life and love of Christ. It is for the contemplative as much as for the apostle to supply this need.

If the contemplative loses sight of the world's labour, ceasing to care for the whole and concentrating only on the part, he contemplates to poor purpose. He may be saving his own soul, but it will be a soul that is shrunk for want of compassion.

The history of religion shows that when Christian mysticism

has been at its best, its exponents have derived their incentive
—after the primary incentive of wanting to give direct worship
to God—from the desire to form Christ in their fellow men.

If the mystic vision is to be kept in right perspective it is
necessary that the mind of the mystic should stick to the
mystic facts. The contemplative must realize that mankind is
all the time being drawn by the power of grace towards the
fulfilment of its destiny in Christ. The end of the world will
come only when the Church has reached full stature in Christ,
and until that moment comes it is for those members of the
human race who are called to the direct service of God by contemplation to further the process. This they do, not virtually
or by implication, but actually and by deliberate intention.

If the trouble in the world has been caused by the drift away
from love, it is for those who are dedicated to love to come
forward with the remedy.

POVERTY OF SPIRIT

POVERTY of spirit is not quite humility and not quite
detachment, but a combination of the two. The importance of the beatitude is shown by the reward which is granted
to the poor of spirit: theirs is the kingdom of heaven. The
reward is not held out in advance; it is enjoyed along with the
poverty. If theirs *is* the kingdom of heaven, then the spirit of
poverty and the spirit of the blessed have a more than casual
affinity. It means that where humility and detachment are
found, there is to be seen the possession of what is fully
possessed in heaven.

Just as the beatific vision will separate us finally from the
drag of created things and from ourselves, so poverty of spirit
is already a separation from creatures and self. What the vow
of poverty legislates for, the spirit of poverty completes. So
comprehensive is the spirit of poverty that, where there has
been no call to religious poverty in the technical sense, the

virtue supplies for the vow. But then you would expect spiritual poverty to be more valuable than temporal poverty.

The voluntary poverty which strips a man of the things that he likes to own is not necessarily spiritual poverty. It may be religious poverty and it may be the best way to acquire the other. But true spiritual poverty does not even like to own. 'The things that were gain to me according to human judgment' says St Paul, 'I have accounted loss.'

A combination of humility and detachment is in flat contradiction to the spirit of the world. The man who is truly poor in spirit cannot be influenced by any of the many forms of worldliness. His heart can never be in projects of ambition, in honours, in luxury, in the vanity of material concerns. His heart is turned away from possessions and passions alike. Impoverished, he is heart-free.

The world is always tied by one or other false value; the poor of spirit have no false values to tie them. 'All that is in the world is the concupiscence of the eyes, the concupiscence of the mind, and the pride of life.' To the other-worldly there are better substitutes for what the eyes, the mind, and the flesh cry out for.

Where worldliness feeds the nerves and in the long run wears them out, poverty of spirit soothes the nerves and in the long run starves them out. In worldliness there is bound to be fear; in poverty of spirit there is no fear because there is nothing to lose. The only thing that the soul fears is the loss of God's love by sin, and even this fear is swallowed up in the trust which the soul places in the power of grace.

If poverty of spirit were a matter of temperament, it would not be a beatitude. There would be no particular merit in acquiring it. But poverty of spirit is more than a natural unassertiveness, more than the meekness which is common among those who for one reason or another are unused to expressing themselves and who are temperamentally unimaginative: it is a gift of the Holy Spirit.

The poor in spirit are the 'weak things of this world who confound the strong', they are the foolish who are wiser than the wise. Their strength and their wisdom come from the Holy Spirit. It is because they are the rich in Spirit that they are bound to be the ones who come up against those who are rich in the flesh, and it must always be the Holy Spirit that wins.

Again it is because poverty of spirit is a supernatural gift of God that it is linked up with the other gifts of God. The truly poor are at the same time truly understanding, truly forgiving, truly wise and truly courageous. Liberty of spirit is made possible by poverty of spirit, and it is liberty of spirit that both crowns and controls the operations of the soul. Liberty of spirit is at once the blessing and channel of love.

The light of the Holy Spirit comes to the soul that is both poor and free, and it is through the soul's poverty and freedom that the light is responded to and the faculties of the soul are exercised according to God. Poverty of spirit and liberty of spirit are not themselves light, but they are habits of soul which most readily discover light. They enable the soul to understand more, to see more, to love more. And understanding, seeing, loving, the soul comes to think less about itself.

The man who is poor in spirit is not bound to people or bored by people. He loves people in charity. His detachment frees him from slavery, and his humility from intolerance. How can a man be tied by blades of grass when his heart is in the hands of God? How can a man be bored by people when he cannot imagine anyone to be more boring than himself? Such a man is on the contrary delighted by the presence of people: they remind him of the charity he owes to God. He is equally delighted by the absence of people: in solitude he is all the more reminded of the charity he owes to God.

So it is that the poverty of spirit which seeks to exclude companionship defeats itself: it shows itself up as being not sufficiently detached from its own poverty and from its own solitude.

True poverty recognizes what is good while denying itself what is unnecessary. False poverty recognizes what is good *only* in the denial of what is unnecessary. The poverty which seeks to destroy, and to find perfection in destruction, is not poverty but anarchy.

In their eagerness to acquire poverty of spirit, souls will be found who try to eliminate their appetites one by one. Each avenue of distraction, they tell themselves, must be blocked. Then they are discouraged because their policy of elimination is seen to bring in more distraction than it suppresses, to cause more struggle than it pacifies, to conjure up images in the mind that are more formidable than those which have been eliminated in the flesh. Such a poverty is not one of spirit: it is merely one of practice, and not a very good one at that.

It would be far better for such souls to learn poverty from the Holy Spirit direct, using the light which God sends to make the renunciations which God wills. Love inspires the detachment which renunciation by itself is sometimes too ruthless to understand.

Where it is the Holy Spirit and not the spirit of self that is regulating the soul's poverty, the renunciations will express themselves according to charity, prudence, humility and obedience. It is only a false poverty, as it is only a false liberty, that plays off one virtue against another. Thus the poverty that is practised against obedience is no holy poverty; nor is that which is arrogant and censorious.

The love of God which binds men to the love of one another does not, in the name of poverty, call men to attack one another. The love of God which places men under authority does not, in the name of poverty, call men to rebel against authority. There are no divisions in the Holy Spirit.

Thus poverty of spirit is a unifying and not a departmental virtue. It is an encompassing virtue. In separating the soul from self and the things of self, it 'comprehends with all the saints' and expands in range and depths with every new demand of grace.

Though poverty of spirit is the element in which other virtues develop, it is itself a virtue which seems not to develop at all. In the case of certain other gifts—the gift of piety, for example, or the gifts of fortitude, justice, mercy—there is something which you can put your finger on and thank God for. But spiritual poverty is elusive: it hides behind its acts and is seen by none. The more interior the poverty, the more blind is the soul to its possession.

Where you find a soul that is increasingly conscious of its own worthlessness and at the same time is increasingly conscious of God's overwhelming mercy, there you find someone who is learning to be poor in spirit. Where you find a soul that is not any longer concerned with self, that considers the sanctification of the world as being more important than its own personal holiness; there you find someone who is truly poor. 'For their sake do I sanctify myself.'

Poverty of spirit is not so much a virtue that produces its characteristic acts as rather a quality whereby all acts are made virtuous. Taking its character from the poverty of Christ, spiritual poverty is the characteristic expression of divine love.

Since Christ, more poor than the foxes or the birds, had nowhere to lay His head, the followers of Christ can hardly fail to make poverty their ideal. And if in these pages the spirit of it has been dealt with to the exclusion of the letter, it is only because the practical side of it is assumed. Also not all who are called to be poor in spirit are called to take the vow of poverty. The beatitude is addressed to the indigent, to the religious, and to the rich alike.

Whether under necessity or under vow or under the general cover of the call to God's service, the soul that is poor has unique claims upon the care of Providence. 'I am poor, and the Lord looks after me' says the psalmist, 'thou art my helper and protector.'

WORK

M AN lives at the level of his desire. If he wants the will of God he gets it, and becomes holy. If he wants the grosser satisfactions he gets them, and becomes gross. If he wants work he can find it; he can be happy in it and be holy in it. But he must not love work too much or he will become a machine.

The man who chooses to make his work an offering to God must avoid the mistakes which men make when they work without reference to God. It is as important to get one's work right as one's prayer. But it is through one's prayer that one's work is given its true character.

The soul of prayer must learn not only what works to do and how to do them, but also when to leave them off. It is only the grace of God received in prayer that can show the soul where the work has got to. The soul must be able to say with Christ 'I have finished the work which thou gavest me to do'.

Until the particular will of God which is the soul's present work has been brought to the close that God wants, it is the will of God that the soul should persevere in it. Not only do it, but perfect it. This means redirecting it where it goes wrong, and constantly pouring more love into it.

If prayer is kept as one activity, and work is kept as another, the only way to judge the work is by its results. And this is no way to judge any work. In the service of God the relationship between prayer and work is of first importance: prayer informs work, and work in turn ministers to prayer.

The wrong orientation of prayer means the wrong orientation of work. If in prayer we look more at self than at God, the work which we do will follow suit. Just as in prayer we have to be constantly pointing our minds towards God and away from self, so in work we have to be forever reminding ourselves why we are working and for whom.

Works which are begun in the spirit have a way of ending in the flesh. Even those works that are the most closely related to the glory of God can be diverted into the service of self. By the same token those works that are distracting and secular can be, but not so easily, supernaturalized.

It is not the character of the work that is the qualification, but the destination. The priest who says Mass with care so as to win the personal approval of the congregation will need to raise the motive of his carefulness. The rubrics of the Mass can look after the action, but they cannot look after the end.

Nor is it necessarily the effort which is put into the work that gives it value. To think that merit is measured by effort or suffering or self-sacrifice would be a mistake. Merit is measured by charity. Effort, suffering, sacrifice—these give proof, not merit.

'The worth of our actions' says St Augustine, 'is what God puts into them.' The only meritorious work is God's. Where He communicates His charity to what we are doing, there and there only is anything valuable to be found in what we do.

Not even the perseverance with which man works is the whole story. Nobody gets to heaven by the power of his endeavour, however sustained. 'My merits are Your wounds': this is the only way anyone gets to heaven.

It is this idea of possessing nothing which one may call one's own in the way of merit that is always uppermost in the minds of those who are poor in spirit. In the extremities of life, as in the ordinary run of every day, it is the only thing that makes for complete dependence upon the mercy of God.

So often it is the surprise and sense of shame at the sight of one's worthlessness that send the soul to the edge of despair. But where the soul is habitually aware of its own misery, and used to relying upon nothing short of God Himself, there is no surprise. There may be shame, but it is taken for granted and less blinding. It is only the blind who despair.

Where a man sees that the whole of his work is conditioned by the action of God, there is little scope for vain elation. The fruitfulness of his labour is God's, not his own. Such a man knows himself to be a steward only, and accountable for the work he is doing. Nor does this take away from the joy of labouring: it adds to it. It does not even take away from the joy of achievement. All it does is to detach the soul from the pride of achievement. There is far more joy in achieving with Christ than in achieving with self.

Souls to whom this truth is a living reality—souls, that is, who are grounded in the virtue of spiritual poverty—may undertake great enterprises for the love of God. Such souls will know that God's glory will be served whether the works succeed or fail.

It is only those who understand how fully their works are God's who can say with St Paul that 'His grace in me has not been void ... by God's grace I am what I am.' It means then that they are learning to take second place.

In giving to God their works, they are not giving *theirs* but *His*. 'These hands that labour' such a soul can say, 'are Yours.' The saint, the mystic, is the one who knows God to be operating through him all the time. To co-operate with this work of God all the time is sanctity. It is also happiness.

Even if the work is one of the bitterest suffering, the fact that the soul is uniting itself with the suffering Christ is happiness. 'I glory in nothing save in the cross of our Lord Jesus Christ.'

The perfection of your work then, as the perfection of your suffering, is the rendering to God what is His in you. This being so, it matters little what sort of work, or what sort of suffering, He happens to want from you. So long as it is His, that is all there is about it.

But what of the choice between works? On what principle am I to act when deciding whether to embark upon a great work and risk it, or to stick to the humble task and play for safety and humility?

As suggested above, there is no limit to the confidence which you may place in God, so provided you place no confidence in your own strength there is nothing which you may not be ready to launch. Your projects will have to be checked by such factors as obedience, suitability to your condition of life, the effect upon other souls, but so far as the work itself goes the more ambitious the better. The ambition is no longer yours but His. The responsibility is no longer yours but His. There can be humbug about this, as there can be humbug about almost everything in the spiritual life, but if you look for the will of God and are reasonably sure that you know what it is, you may take up the most formidable works without a tremor.

If there is one disadvantage to the doctrine of doing little things for God, it is that you get out of the way of doing big things for God. Nobody will deny that fidelity to the commonplace is sanctifying, but what sort of holiness is it that shies away from the highest opportunity on the grounds that lowliness is better?

Granted that the opportunity comes from God, the rejection of the opportunity is more likely to spring from fear than from humility. There is no better disguise for fear and laziness than the edifying desire not to push oneself forward.

Little acts of love are pleasing to God: if the present century has learned nothing else about the service of God it has learned that much. But the size of the act is relative; love is the significant factor.

Generosity is not giving to God this or that work, this or that suffering, this or that prayer; it is giving to God the most love that it is in one's power to give at the moment. This assumes everything—including the will to persevere in this same state of giving.

Wrongly conceived, the cult of littleness can turn true heroism upside down and will see a new and loftier martyrdom in the enduring of pinpricks.

Rightly conceived, the way of littleness responds with simplicity to heroic endeavours and the unforseeable martyrdoms of grace. It is simplicity, which is itself the outcome of poverty of spirit, which makes possible the harmony of such opposites as ambition and humility. Simplicity makes this harmony possible because it makes it unselfconscious.

Simplicity sees the work to be done, and the Person for whom it is to be done. Simplicity hardly looks at the self who is called upon to do it. Simplicity does not ask 'Am I justified? Dare I venture?' The only relevant question is 'Does God want it?'—and if He does, the bigger it is the better.

It would be a good thing, both for spiritual literature in general and for authors individually, if spiritual writers decided to write only *big* books. Not necessarily long books, but books about big things. It would be a good plan if preachers in the same way preached only on enlarging themes instead of on

III

subtle fancies. The gospel is big enough: let men write and preach about that.

Besides the balance to be kept between ambition and humility, there is another balance which spiritual people must maintain in their work for God. It is the harmony of action and contemplation. Contemplatives are too often afraid that the least activity will cause distraction and involve them in endless misery; souls in the active life, afraid of wasting their time, are suspicious of contemplation.

What the contemplative has to realize is that the existence of active duties in his life is not an obstacle to his vocation: an obstacle to his vocation is the non-existence of contemplation.

What the active soul has to realize is that time spent in prayer is not time taken away from his works of charity: the thing that takes away from works of charity is not enough prayer.

Where the contemplative makes the mistake of thinking that the atmosphere of prayer is everything, the active makes the mistake of thinking that the accumulation of works is everything. What both of them need to know is that the love of God is everything.

The principle in either case is the same: work must be the outcome of prayer. But notice that it is the prayer that gives the form to the work, and not the work that gives the form to the prayer. Work is the will of God, but it is in prayer that the soul comes to see it as such.

If God is in the prayer, then God will be in the work. God may not be divided. It is not a choice between prayer *or* work; it is a choice of prayer *and* work. Prayer finds expression in work; work finds inspiration and direction in prayer. In prayer, as in work, it is *caritas Christi urget nos* : not two activities but one.

Revelation does not tell us that God is prayer or that God is work. Revelation tells us that God is love. Where divine charity is truly the force behind the activity, it does not greatly matter whether love is fulfilling itself in acts of prayer or in acts of zeal.

Allowing that the act of loving God in prayer is more direct than the act of loving Him through the service of His creatures, the practical question is always how best to relate the two. The sanctification of work by prayer can be looked at from different points of view. Either you can lay the stress on the actual exercise of prayer which precedes the work, or you can take the work as being so charged with the will of God that you are praying implicitly, and at times explicitly, while you are performing it. The first says a prayer over the typewriter and then gets down to work, the second lets the prayer come up through the keys.

Love tends to unity. 'Through love,' as the Mass of Christ the King reminds us, 'He has drawn all things to Himself.' For a man who is thus drawn into the unity of God's creation, it should not be too difficult to decide either how much activity may be allowed into his life or the degree to which he may give himself to it. His prayer will show him the order to be observed. 'In Thy light I shall see light.'

Such a soul will know that he may not think of a holiness apart from his work or in spite of his work, but that he must think of it as emerging from his work and because of it. He has a single vocation in which there is no conflict of ideals.

The saint does not say 'I am for the interior life' or 'I am for the apostolate': he says 'I am for God', and lets God arrange the particular drift of his life. Nor does he say 'I am for the liturgy' or 'I am for solitary prayer': he knows that they amount to the same thing. Nor does he say 'I am for suffering' or 'I am for holy joy': he welcomes either in the singleness of his surrender.

In the last analysis it is what God wills that matters, and this is the whole story as regards a man's work. To let God choose it for him, to let God work it through him, to let God have its outcome: there is nothing more a man need know about the principle of work.

FOR the religious the problem of what works to undertake is not so difficult as for the soul living in the world: for the religious there is the vow of obedience, there is the spirit of the house to which he belongs, there is the tradition of his order. For a religious to force his undertaking past any of these, even with the necessary permissions at the back of him, is to work for self and not for God.

But allowing that there are occasions when the choice of work is left to the individual, there are certain general principles which can act as a guide to the interior soul whether religious or lay. The principles are necessarily very general because almost always there are particular factors, economic or domestic or to do with health and age, which call for *ad hoc* direction. Some of what follows may be, in certain cases, impossible of application. The phrase here, as frequently elsewhere in laying down spiritual principle, is 'all things being equal'.

The first practical aim for the man of prayer with regard to his work is to get his life balanced. Not only must he not exist for the sake of his work, but he must not allow his work to disturb the proportion of his day: his energy has to be distributed: the prayer life and the life of fraternal charity have to be considered.

The balance, moreover, must extend beyond the day to the year: a work involving weeks or months of intense application followed by stretches of idleness disturbs the evenness which is necessary for contemplative prayer. Thus if a man's work is that of teaching or preaching or studying in a university, an additional work must be found which will keep him occupied during the intervals.

The life of sanctity is one of constant movement towards God. The saint who becomes static ceases to be a saint. The contemplative who thinks he has come far enough in contemplation is no contemplative. To come to a halt in the search after union with God, even if the halt is intended to be only temporary, is to show that the intention, whatever it was at the beginning, is not entirely serious. It shows that the soul has been experimenting merely.

When a man surrenders himself to God, he surrenders his leisure as well as his life. The vocation to surrender assumes the vocation to prayer and work. Consequently if prayer and work are bound up with a man's sanctity there must be no dropping out. Both prayer of some sort and work of some sort must be unremitting in the life of the man who is in earnest about following his call to lifelong service of God.

Caritas Christi urget nos: it does so not in spurts but in the exercise of constant pressure. If the pressure can be the same pressure so much the better. But because most souls find it impossible to persevere without changes of some sort, even holidays of some sort, in their lives, a system must be worked out whereby a continuity of pressure is maintained.

The contemplative will need to plan his replacements carefully if he is not to be involved in sterility and sloth. He should find that by a judicious process of exchanges he can reduce his holidays to the minimum. The need for recreation is not the same in everybody, but the desire to recreate seems pretty universal. It is the desire that sometimes over-presents the need.

It would perhaps be too severe to say categorically that interior souls should never give themselves periods of rest. There may be times of enforced inactivity, as for example when recovering from an illness or being moved from one work to another, and there may even be times when it is conscientiously judged that the work itself is suffering for want of the soul's relaxation. In such cases a holiday is presumably the only way of meeting the situation. The inactivity is enforced by circumstance: the holiday is chosen with reluctance. But whether submitted to or chosen, the holiday, once its necessity is agreed upon, may be enjoyed as coming from God.

Such questions have to be decided on their individual merits. But this in general we can certainly claim: in order to live at the highest level of Christian life there has to be the discipline of labour. Work is laid upon man as an ascesis, and requires not only fidelity to the principle of self-denial but also method and routine. Where there is no framework there will be laxity instead of liberty of spirit.

Souls need to be responsible to an observance, and without a fixed and punctual attendance they will find that their prayer suffers, their charity becomes social and selective, and their penance peters out altogether. Granted that the interior life is not designed for the sake of the timetable but the timetable for the sake of the interior life, the only antidote to that weariness of welldoing which is described by the ancients under the heading of *accedia* is constancy to the commitments.

If the problem of work for interior souls were merely one of providing occupation there would be no great difficulty. But it is also one of providing interest. A man is meant to be pleased with, and in, the work that he does for God. His work is meant to afford him just the kind of happiness which his nature needs: it is a derivative happiness but a true and God-intended happiness nevertheless.

A man may legitimately expect to find interest in the work of imparting the things of God, in study, in artistic creation, in works of mercy. If he expects to find interest only in secular affairs and worldly diversions he will either vegetate from sheer disgust in the spiritual sphere or else scatter his energies over the wide field of mundane opportunity. It is important to look for your interests as coming from inside and not outside your vocation.

There is likely to be an element of self in all this, but the possibility must be risked. If you deliberately exclude all interest in your work, doing only the works which have no appeal for you, you go against a law of your nature which can normally be taken to represent the will of God.

It is a mistake to ask yourself whether you are interested in the work because you do it well, or whether you do it well because you are interested in it. Do it for God and forget about everything else.

Besides, who except only the greatest saints would be able to exclude self-interest from works of administration, creative art, the moulding of young people? Even in works as impersonal as those of hidden scholarship, official correspondence, anonymous research, there must be—and there are meant to be—incentives which are subsidiary to the ruling motive which is supernatural.

So far as the danger of self-interest goes, it is greater for the contemplative who plunges himself into active work than for the active who plunges himself in contemplative work. The contemplative can perhaps do more good but he can also do more harm. The active who is engaged in contemplative occupations stands to gain more and to lose less.

In following up a new interest the contemplative is more likely to be swept off his feet than the active. When the contemplative takes it into his head to rescue souls by direct influence he is apt to consume them instead of serve them. His zeal runs away with him. He is not, as the active is, conditioned to the distraction involved.

The impulse on the part of a contemplative towards active work is one that has to be looked at closely. The occasion calls for clear thinking and statement of policy. The unfortunate part about it is that the contemplative's friends are hardly ever any help. If he is not under a superior or enlightened director he will have to judge God's will by the light of prayer alone. And souls have a way of playing about with this light.

The contemplative who is thinking of widening his sphere of influence will be told how sensible he is to come out into the open at last and help so many who would not otherwise learn of the things of God. But if he is called to the contemplative life he will be foolish to listen to such talk. He is in danger of emptying his spiritual life and filling up his heart again with what he has given up.

The active soul who knows what his vocation involves is in a happier state: for him to perfect his technique, not to change it. What the active soul has to do is to perform his active works in the spirit of contemplation. The ideal for him is not to stop work in order to pray, nor yet to stop prayer in order to work, but to bring the two closer together so that they come to mean one thing.

Whether for the contemplative or for the active soul, then, the aim is the same: it is a question as to where you start from rather than a question as to what you do or even how successfully you do it. If love is the ideal in the mind of the contemplative and active alike, the labels can be dropped. There is no great point in such labels anyway.

Though there is no work that cannot be spiritualized by prayer so that it becomes a prayer, the work which is almost a prayer already—and the one in which there is least room for self—is manual labour.

The man who works in God's presence under the sky learns more of God's universe than he learns from books. Manual labour gives him the same sense of the universality of God's purpose as he might get from a study of antiquity. But to absorb the knowledge from nature is one better than to absorb it from the story of successive civilizations. History brings him at one remove what he may learn direct from creation.

To derive value from working out of doors and on the soil you must make more than a hobby of it: your manual labour must be salted with austerity. There is nothing against fancy gardening as an outlet, but it does not do for the soul what regular manual labour does. Sitting in a deckchair does not do it either.

The man who allows his body to be weathered with the changes of climate and season, who tries to keep recollected while he works, who cherishes the silence and solitude which his manual labour affords him as something sacred to God, comes to enjoy deep interior peace. He acquires a certain complicity with creation, and this leads him in turn to closer union with the Creator.

To the objection that time spent in manual labour is a waste of more useful employment, it must be insisted that far from being a drag on other works it gives impetus to them. Intellectual and creative work are all the better for the ideas which, consciously or unconsciously, are absorbed during the monotonous hours in the open and which come to the surface when they are wanted later on. Preaching, writing, teaching are likely to be airless if quite unassociated with the elemental things.

You might imagine that a period spent daily in solitary labour among cabbages and tree-trunks would perhaps, even if it cannot be for more than an hour or two a day, isolate a man from others and reflect upon his charity. But not at all. Experience shows that sympathy with material creation widens rather than narrows the soul's sympathy with living beings. The Spirit of God is more clearly felt to be blowing through the whole of his created effect.

To the man who is in harmony with the courses and rhythms of nature, to the man who mounts from the visible to the invisible and sees by means of his prayer and work the temporal in terms of the eternal, inanimate creation seems not to be so inanimate after all: God has breathed over it and it is still warm. Rational creation for its part is felt to be more than ever rational, God having His reasons for its existence and man rationally responding to His will. The soil need be no barrier to the social obligation.

If there is an error to be guarded against by those who work on the land it might be a certain intolerance, not with other workers but with other works. The feeling can grow that the only appropriate activity for the religious man is field labour, and that sophistication is all nonsense.

As a corrective to the hot-house intellectualism of the age— emphasizing the truth that the basic education of man, the most elemental culture, is that of agriculture—the lauding of husbandry is no bad thing. But it must not be made a fetish.

Man can turn anything into an idolatry. He can make a mysticism out of a mood. Always, and the more so when life is felt to be becoming increasingly complex, the idea of the simple life will have its appeal. But in our march back to the land we must make sure that we are marching with the right intention. The ground which we tread is no holier than God makes it, and we may not canonize the rustic for being a rustic. Such is the power of our self-deception that we can dig the red earth for years for no better reason than that of seeing ourselves with the hardened toil-worn hands of the labourer: we prefer this picture to that of the man at the desk with the typewriter.

In the work of man's hands, whether skilled or unskilled, whether of craft or of art, there are balances to be maintained. There is nothing that so easily upsets the balance as the picturesque or the partisan. If the purpose of the work is the glory of God then neither doctrinaire considerations nor considerations of glamour may find a place.

Manual labour, like silence and solitude and regular observance, is a means only and not something to be deified. But like silence and solitude and regular observance it is a means which the spiritual man cannot afford to be scornful about: it is sanctified by a tradition which is older than the choir, the enclosure, the vows of religion.

'If a man will not work, then neither let him eat': work is evidently man's justification for continuing to live. If he will not work he will be a dead weight on the community: he may not batten on the supplies of the mystical body. So long as he works he can find God in his work; and he can also find himself. He finds charity too, for if he is working according to God he is helping in the communion of saints.

'As a rock in the storm of the sea, so is the persistent work of a man's hands.' In labour, unexciting and unnoticed, a soul may find a spirituality which will lead him in the company of some of the greatest earlier and later saints—but mostly earlier —to God. Not for nothing was St Peter a fisherman, St Paul a tentmaker, and our Lord Himself a carpenter.

THE SAINTS

THE ideal of the Christian soul is that God's will should stand for so much in his life that in following it he comes to resemble Christ with whom his whole purpose is identified

The saint may never rest in anything short of that. To stop short is to restrict the response to grace, and for sanctity the response must be as complete as it is constant.

Does this mean that the saint never sins? No, it means that the saint never tires of trying not to. Does it mean that the saint is always at the top of his power in the activity of loving God? No, it means he is always wanting to be.

Sanctity is a condition of heart which may fail again and again in its ideal but which is in constant renewal. Its uninterrupted purpose of wanting God expresses itself in acts, and, when fully informed by grace, becomes itself an act. It is like the numberless photographs of a film becoming a single moving picture: the acts of perfection are so continuous in the soul of the saint as to become an ever-present activity, and so a habit.

For the ordinary Christian as for the saint, God is the ideal. The Catholic who goes to Mass on Sundays will admit that, when you get down to it and face the essentials, it is God alone that matters. The saint knows this too, but will not let it rest at that. The saint takes that one single piece of truth and expands it to its fullest implication.

To one man God is the terminus *a quo* and *ad quem;* to the other God is the sum of his happiness. To one man God is the means of his attaining to heaven when he dies; to the other He is the whole end of his desire whether in this life or the next. One man will allow that God has first claim on him but at the same time allows other claims which he wants to see satisfied in his life; another man has God's claim always before his eyes and takes care that there should be no room in his life for any other. The saint is the one whose allegiance is habitually single.

Though the saint, unlike the other man, has nothing in his life that is not God's, he is not on that account forever preoccupied with the thought of what, in order to maintain that state, he may next be called upon to renounce. Saints are not people who are constantly discovering new things to give to God, new horrors to inflict upon themselves, new worlds to conquer for Him. They are people who let God take, who let

Him arrange the matter of suffering, who let Him do the conquering.

The real reason why grace holds undisputed sway over the soul of the saint is not so much that the soul is empty of attachments and self-interest as that it is full of the desire to love. What makes the saint different from the ordinary man is simply this: he is possessed by the will of God not only because he has offered himself to fulfil it as perfectly as he can but because it is for him the only reality. There are many who offer themselves to fulfil God's will, but few to whom it is the whole significance of life.

It is because the essential difference between the saint and the rest of men is something interior, something confined to a way of looking at God and the things of God, that you can know the saint only in some of his acts. The external effects of a man's attitude of mind can help you to form a judgment—you know the tree by its fruits—but they do not give the whole story. You come to think of the essence of sanctity in terms of the external: you become so fascinated by the manifestations of sanctity that you forget what they come from.

Acts of sanctity do not spring from heroism but from grace. Heroism is a quality which we can grasp, which has a ring about it, which we know to be connected with fixity of purpose, so we look for it in the saint. The operation of grace in the soul holds less interest for us. But nothing except grace can make a man a saint.

Neither knowledge nor zeal nor industry nor endurance can make a man a saint. But it is either knowledge or zeal or industry or endurance that we recognize about the saints. So we mistake the cause and effect.

Because we can imagine types of sanctity, reconstruct the specific sanctity of individual saints, know all about the various signs of sanctity, we tend to miss the actual sanctity that is being lived in the world around us. This would not matter so much if it did not lead us to regard saints as belonging to a different dimension of spirituality from the one to which we are trying to accustom ourselves.

We have to be constantly reminding ourselves that the prepared environment of the saints is the same as the prepared environment in which we have to live out our own lives. And that the whole thing depends upon whether we meet it surrendering at every point to the action of grace which is our only sanctity or whether we insist on hewing out a sanctity of our own which is no sanctity at all.

Saints are not those who have won their way to the topmost pinnacles: they are those who have lost their way in the back streets, following after Christ whom they are always just missing. But they have not in fact missed Him, for He lost all and they bear their loss with Him.

So saints do not become saints by being either successful or unsuccessful. They become saints by being united to Christ. It is only then that they become themselves. God meant them to become saints all along, and until they do they fall short of their own identity.

No man arrives at sanctity by the fact of having done things perfectly: he does things perfectly by the fact of having co-operated with grace. A man cannot, in the Christian sense, suffer perfectly or love perfectly—or indeed do anything perfectly—unless he is united with Christ from whom his perfection derives. It is a question of facts, not a question of feeling heroic and generous. A man cannot live up to feeling heroic and generous unless Christ puts it in him to do so.

How can we be any longer surprised at the humility of the saints? Could they very well have been anything else? They saw, habitually and in a way which we see only at the rarest intervals, that it really *is* by the grace of God that saints can be what they are. *Quia fecit mihi magna qui potens est*: it is He who does it; it is I who let Him.

It is easy enough to think of the blessed in heaven finding their fulfilment in God: we assume that desire is so rarified by then that God is their whole happiness. What puzzles us, knowing what we do of ourselves, is the idea that God can be everything to people on earth. But He can be or He would not be the reason for their existence.

Man exists only because God is. The sole reason why man has life at all, and why he has this particular life to live, is that God has a life of His own which He wants man to share with Him. Man has no other meaning, no other reason for continuing to exist. I am alive because I am His: I am His because He wants me: I keep on being alive because He wants me all the time: if He ceased to want me I should cease to be.

A painter has a picture in his mind before he paints it. There is no picture on the canvas; it is in his head. Nothing to show for the picture until the artist applies the colours. The artist may want, more than anything else in the world, to see his picture before his eyes; but if he does not paint it there will be nothing to see. With God it is different: His *fiat* brings being.

The painter starts on his picture. The picture is kept going by the desire, the creative idea, of the painter. But only until it is finished. When the picture is what the artist wanted to produce, the desire and the picture part company: become two different things. The picture has an existence of its own. In the case of God and the soul it is exactly the reverse: the soul not only depends for its existence upon the continued desire for it in the mind of God but draws closer into union with God in the measure that it faithfully reflects what it was in the mind to create.

To have painted his picture the artist has had to collect materials. 'For this picture' he has said, 'I want plenty of chrome and a flat brush.' God has not wanted material, He has wanted me; and the desire alone has produced me. Take away from the finished picture the paint and the canvas: what is left? Nothing. Take away from me the continued desire which God has for me, and what is left? Nothing. The painter sells his picture, forgets about it, takes up music and never gives his creation another thought. What happens to the picture? It goes on being a picture.

How can I go on being a soul if I am not incessantly in the thought of God, in God's desire? If I am to be a Christian in any full sense, if I am to be a saint, the thing that will help me most in my way to God will be the knowledge that but for

God's ever-supporting love there would be nothing to support. At every moment of time I am wanted by God with all His will.

With *all* His will? Me? What of His will with regard to others, with regard to before and after my time on earth? What of His will in relation to matters of which I shall never have any knowledge? His will for the planets, for the stars, for the seasons ... how can the whole of this will be focused upon me?

God is undivided, and where He wills and loves He wills and loves with the whole of Himself. Just as though I were the isolated instance of His creative thought, the one person whom He had planned, I receive the full force of God's love.

To the saint, living in the awareness of this truth, there is nothing strange about God's readiness to forgive sin, to answer prayer, to work miracles, to lavish graces irrespective of merit. The saint knows he deserves nothing in the way of favours: if it were a question of his merit he would never ask for anything. But knowing God's love for him, the saint leans on the Beloved's love. He dares, realizing that it is God's own love within him that gives him the desire and the power, to love back.

The saint, never losing his own identity but on the contrary discovering it, identifies himself ever more completely with the life of Christ. There is nothing in this of feeling himself to be a superior Christian: 'superior' and 'inferior' are meaningless when applied to identification. The saint knows that it is only because God dwells in him that he sees the created order in God's terms: it is God in him that recognizes God outside him. It is God in him that loves God in other people. It is God in him that bows to the will of God. Back once again to 'I live, now not I, but Christ liveth in me.'

In the order of nature it may be true that a subject cannot be its own object. But Aristotle was not allowing for the order of grace, where God is at once the lover and the loved, the caller and the called. Even the saint may not find God as he wants to find Him, but it is God inside the saint who is conducting the search. It is God in him who is the seeker and the sought.

'The soul loves God' says St John of the Cross, 'not through itself but through Him ... it loves through the Holy Spirit, even as the Father and the Son love one another.'

God is present not as possessed in the soul but as possessing the soul; not as contained in the soul but as containing the soul; not as depending upon the soul's realization of the fact of grace, but as the fact and grounds of the soul's dependence upon grace.

In all this we must guard against error. Revealing ever-deeper implications as the doctrine of the indwelling does—nor is it merely a tenable theory of mystical speculation but is given by theologians as a fact of grace—it is sometimes understood in the wrong sense. It may not be presented with a pantheistic twist. The essential otherness of God must always be remembered: the soul is given a share in the life of God, not in His essence. But this share is not metaphorical, it is real.

Real though the relationship is, it can be only imperfectly realized in this life, only known by inference. In heaven man's happiness is to know God—just as on earth it is man's happiness to know God—but with the beatific vision the knowledge is unimpaired. In heaven the soul knows not any more by analogy and association, not any more by abstraction and derivation, but by what theologians, greatly daring, call 'possession'. Then, and only then, is the transformation complete.

But even here on earth man may begin to learn: and learning —love. Man must experience here in order that he may experience there. Though the sanctity of a soul is crowned in heaven, it is shaped on earth.

While a man is still confined to the limits of his being he sees the things of God, himself included, as in a glass—obscurely. Not until he sees God face to face will he find an explanation of the things of God, himself included. In the meantime he sees by faith, knowing that as a glove is meant for the hand that wears it, as a love-letter is meant for the eye that reads it, as an absolution is meant for the penitent that asks for it, so he is meant for God. Uncertain perhaps of his own true nature till the last day of his life, the soul can grow in likeness to Christ hidden. 'If you had not already found Me you would not now be searching for Me' ... if you had not always sought for Me, you would not now have lost yourself.

Few have known more of sanctity than St John of the Cross, and with him the paradox comes almost as a refrain: when I am lost, then am I found. It is thus that the saint touches reality in this life, for how else could he live by faith? It will be different when he comes to rest in the knowledge which all his lifetime he has secretly acquired: 'This is eternal life that they should know Thee, and Jesus Christ whom Thou hast sent.'

CONTEMPLATION

JUST as the sanctity of the saints is not their own but is a sanctity borrowed from the sanctity of God—*Tu solus sanctus*—so the contemplation of contemplatives is not their own but is what they are allowed to receive of God's contemplation of Himself. That is why the soul's act of contemplation is one of taking in rather than one of giving out.

In the sense that it is never idle, the act of contemplation is active. In the sense that it is always yielding, it is passive. Contemplation is the habit born of the extended act, at once deliberate and receptive. It is the disposition to contemplate: it is the state of positive acquiescence.

The specific act of contemplation is the exercise of love expressed either in the liturgy or in the prayer of faith. The environment or normal habitat of contemplation is abstraction of life. Contemplation, whether seen as the habit or its act, is a grace.

Contemplation is not the conscious beholding of God, but the directing of the soul towards God. It is the recognition rather than the vision of God. The vision of God is for the blessed in heaven: contemplatives on earth have to be content with the joys and the labours of stretching out towards Him.

Contemplation as practised by souls in this life is the constant, serene, experimental, loving—though not emotional or continuously actual—appreciation of God as the fulfilment of love.

We have seen on an earlier page that to the saint God is not one of many claimants upon his love but is all his love. To the soul who is seriously trying to serve God in contemplative prayer, but who is by no means yet a saint, there may be other claimants but their claim is resented and opposed. There is a growing conviction in the soul that to love other things and God simultaneously is an anomaly.

The contemplative knows that good things are lovable, and that good people love them. But he knows too that if he himself is to be launched on the contemplative way to God, there must be no simultaneous loving. The contemplative sees what the ideal for him is, even if he cannot see how he is to live according to it. His contemplation will teach him how.

Nor does the contemplative greatly worry about the means by which he will attain to the union for which he craves. He knows that since he is made for God, and has no meaning apart from this purpose, the effecting of the union, as also the degree of union to which he is admitted, can be left to God. He knows that it will be in the meeting of his soul and God that not only his own desire but God's as well—that creative desire of God's by which the soul exists—are fulfilled.

Perhaps the chief difference between the soul who practises contemplative prayer and the soul who practises discursive prayer is this: in the one God is felt to be the centre of gravity, in the other the soul itself is felt to be the centre and the motive force. The knowledge of God possessed by contemplatives is therefore more direct: it no longer has to be learned through the medium of its own power.

If to be a Christian is to have access to the knowledge of God in this life through Christ—'he that seeth Me seeth the Father'—then to be a contemplative is to enjoy this knowledge in the fullest and most direct sense. The light which his more immediate prayer gives to the contemplative puts him on the way towards enjoying the truest perception of God attainable on earth.

It is not study or natural intuition that perceives God, but grace. This is the specific grace of contemplation, carrying the soul through to the closest union of love. The level of reality at which a contemplative lives is a hidden one: mysticism means no more than that.

Since serenity is of the essence of contemplation it must be safeguarded. Though coming more as an effect than as a cause, serenity is the climate of the contemplative knowledge of God. Though having more of an interior than an exterior value, serenity has to be cultivated by means of the senses. The exterior senses first of all, and then the interior senses.

Though the normal environment in which the contemplative knowledge of God is acquired is solitude, the word of God is not bound: it can be spoken to the soul in any place and at any time and against any noise. But for the practice of contemplative prayer there is nothing better than the contemplative life: it would be foolish to imagine that the contemplative life had been designed for anything else.

Since there are contemplative souls following active vocations, and active souls following contemplative vocations, it is idle to speculate on the way in which the Holy Spirit proceeds in the matter. Granted that the vocation to either life comes from God, and that the particular form of living has not been taken up as an escape, the issue is perfectly clear: both the contemplative and active vocations carry with them the grace of potential union.

There is a difference between the contemplative's and the active's response to existing circumstances. Where the contemplative whose vocation calls him to activity must be careful not to spend himself on the setting, the active soul whose vocation calls him to the contemplative life must do the reverse: he must give himself to the setting and thus make good what he lacks in the way of inward solitude.

The active soul, by fidelity to the prepared condition of contemplation in which he finds himself by the terms of his vocation, purifies his prayer and disposes himself for the grace of contemplation; the contemplative, by fidelity to the interior activity of contemplation, purifies his exterior obligations and disposes himself for the transforming union which will settle him in his essential vocation.

Thus the problem for the contemplative soul called to the mixed life of action and contemplation is not so immediate as that of the active soul called to contemplation: the one has the light of his prayer to help him, the other has the conflict between his attraction and his nature to hinder him. Where the contemplative has to be encouraged to follow the drawing of grace which is now almost second nature, the active soul has to be encouraged to brush aside the prejudices of reason and the promptings of sense.

The active soul on the threshold of contemplation is exposed to attack. Would you not expect the devil to make every effort to turn such a soul away from such a good? The devil will use humility, fear of delusion, conscientious devotion to duty, and even charity itself in order to deter the soul from walking in a more interior way of life.

The active soul would accordingly do wrong to steer away from contemplative prayer on the grounds that under existing circumstances it would be presumption to practise it. Allowing that contemplative prayer is God's gift, a grace which may be aspired to but not merited, it is not presumption to put yourself in the way of getting it. It would be much more of a responsibility to put yourself out of the way of getting it.

The soul who feels interiorly uncomfortable in the ways of discursive prayer, and who at the same time would like to give himself to the exercise of waiting silently upon God, must be ruthless in sweeping away doctrinaire objections: the only rule for such a soul is to make straight for what the spirit tells him of God, and to pray in the way that loves most and works best.

Obstacles to embarking upon a more interior prayer come chiefly from two misconceptions. These, quite apart from the false reasoning suggested by the devil and already referred to, re quite enough to divert an active soul into further activity when all along he is being given the chance of deeper recollection. The first misconception is to imagine that the authorities who write about contemplation are unintelligible; the other is to think of the contemplative life as unlivable.

It is in the providence of God that to those souls who are called to practise contemplative prayer, the books, which to others are obscure, become luminously clear when read with simplicity and a serious desire for enlightenment. Indeed it may be taken as one of the signs that the soul is genuinely called to contemplative prayer: the soul will feel an instinctive response to the doctrine of true spirituality.

To know beyond all doubt that what one reads is in exact conformity with what one experiences gives a satisfaction which is beyond that of sense and study: it is a satisfaction to which the novice in contemplation is entitled. Later on, when the night of the spirit comes down upon the soul, this particular confirmation will be withdrawn. But the soul may make the most of it while it lasts.

The second misconception—that of judging the contemplative life to be beyond all ordinary living—is more significant: it makes out the contemplative to be a psychological rarity. The error in all this is that no allowance is made for the working of grace.

It is true that contemplation is beyond nature. It is true that the contemplative lives on a plane which is not the same as other men's. Admit the love of God and the power of God, and these adjustments to the supernatural are not so difficult to understand.

In the spiritual order there is nothing necessarily extraordinary about the contemplative's prayer. Nor in the physical order is there anything peculiar about his life. It is simply that both his prayer and his life are being trained by grace to a fuller experience of reality. He is learning more about truth.

St Augustine says that contemplation directs the soul's tranquil gaze towards those things that supremely are'. There is nothing freakish about this. It is what everybody ought to be doing. True, to hold the gaze thus directed requires the operation of grace, but so it does also to begin with the work of directing. Without the grace of God we cannot so much as call upon the name of Jesus.

Contemplatives and mystics should not then be thought of as the rare experts, religion's proudest exceptions, but more as the common examples which God is wanting many souls to follow. To those who will look at these examples with a practical and generous eye, God will give light to show what to do next.

Far from wafting through life in a haze of holy transport, the contemplative is more alive than most to human needs. Certainly, as will be seen in the next section, he knows that he may not scorn them. Nor does he merely tolerate life as an inevitable, but disagreeable, waiting-room necessity. Instead he experiences life. He is the only one who really does.

CHARITY

WE love God not in our dreams or reasonings, but in our relationships with Him and with our neighbour. It is only too possible for the contemplative to focus attention upon only one aspect of charity—the part which relates to God direct—and to assume that the other is implicitly served.

Noble sentiments about God, lofty conceptions of sacrifice, a planned austerity: these things are of value only where there is already the reality. *Deus caritas est.* God is not prayer or penance or even humility but love. Charity does not point the way to God, nor is it a substitute for God in this life or the best way of pleasing God. Charity *is* God. 'He who abides in charity abides in God, and God in him.'

If for the soul there is no alternative to God in this life then there is no alternative to love. Because God is one, love is one: man may not divide the honours and decide which outweighs the other. 'I am the way, the truth, the life' ... and I am love. The mysticism that knows only one love in Christ, His love for the Father, is not seeing Christ in unity but in division: it is leaving out Christ's love for man. It is no true mysticism that does this.

There are souls who love God with all their might, or think they do, and who take only a patronising interest in the charity which affects their neighbour. The contemplative who recognizes the need for Christian charity—as indeed he can hardly help doing—but who looks upon it as the elementary part of his formation in love, as a very ordinary sort of thing compared with what he is practising in his contemplation, is no true contemplative.

The contemplative may know all about loving God in his neighbour and loving his neighbour in God, but unless he puts this knowledge to practical effect his contemplation is dead. And a dead love is worse than a love unborn.

If the contemplative's purpose is to learn Christ, he of all men should know where Christ is most likely to be found, most likely to be learned. In man the Incarnation is unendingly repeated: 'You are Christ's, and Christ is God's.' Christ is born in all men, and all men are born in Him. If the Father looks for Christ in men, and receives them in virtue of Christ, then we too must look for Christ in men and receive them in virtue of Christ.

Why is it that when we have said all this, and known it for the truth, we still draw back? Is the Christ-life which we have received in baptism so weak in us that His love has never come out into the open? Have we hidden it inside ourselves behind that wall of indifference which is part of our pre-baptismal self? Have we allowed nature to form a crust over the best that humanity, taken simply as humanity, has got to offer?

Some people are so severe by nature that something from outside has to break in and discover what nature has been hiding. They are like coconuts which have to be knocked hard before you can get at what is inside. When their lives, their self-esteem, their 'defence mechanisms' are lying about in pieces, such souls become at last humble and kind.

A person's exterior need bear no necessary relation to his

interior. There may be a wealth of humanity locked up in a quite human heart; but none of this is much good to charity unless the particular pressure is removed which keeps the doors and windows shut. The pressure is nearly always fear.

For most people the humanity which is in them has to be born of suffering. Few are so loving that charity is second nature. Even those who are naturally charitable have to suffer if their charity is to grow into supernatural compassion.

The daylight that has to be let into the souls of contemplative people if they are not to grow stale and sterile in their darkness is so bright that it blinds. It is not seen at first as charity, as humanity, as the soul's part in the Incarnation. It is not seen as a good at all. It may even be seen as a temptation.

The contemplative whose spirituality is at all off-centre is so used to looking in one direction, and in one direction only, that when either a grace or a suffering comes from the other direction it is not understood. It is seen in reverse.

But the love that is in the contemplative must come out into the air somehow, so God arranges in His Providence that the doors creak back on their rusty hinges, and the windows rend their cobwebs. But the process is painful to the soul: there is nothing more agonizing than to see what you conceive to be your only defences being ruthlessly scrapped. You are exposed at last.

But even bearing the above in mind, we should know that it harms charity less to be inhibited by reserve than diluted by sentiment. The talent which is buried under misconceived severity can be dug up and used: the talent which is squandered by misconceived affection is no longer there to be used.

Sentimentality sugars over the sacrificial side of charity, and so hides its essential expression. Like every other virtue charity has to be preserved against a false conception of itself, against a self-portrait which is a caricature.

Precisely because charity is so all-important, the obstacles to charity are so numerous and subtle. Precisely because the horizon of love is so wide, the area of self-deception is so fertile.

Thus we can love the works of charity not because they

relate to God, or even because they relate to people, but because they relate to self. Self-love can make a man embrace lepers, give alms, do deeds of high heroism. All the finest fruits of charity, the virtues deriving from charity, can be turned inside out and made to serve self.

Where self dictates the terms of charity, ordering the works to be performed in the name of charity, there can be only pride in whatever is the outcome.

As in the case of manual labour where we can spoil the supernatural work by seeing ourselves as humble sons of toil, as in the case of prayer where we can see ourselves as souls of silent contemplation kneeling rigid for long hours before the Blessed Sacrament or in the stillness of the cell, as in the case of penance where we can see ourselves as rugged ascetics schooled to the merciless treatment of our bodies while at the same time extending a gentle consideration for the frailties of man, so in the case of charity we can look in the looking glass and see the tireless helpers of the sick, the ready benefactors of the poor, the patient visitors of the imprisoned.

But what sort of a charity is it that either dramatises itself for its own benefit or that throws its virtue into relief for the edification of others? Is there generosity in giving when the credit for the gift is prized beyond the purpose of the giving?

Mercy, compassion, hospitality, willingness to help: these qualities must be pruned or they will grow twisted and away from the parent stem of charity. Charity must not come to resemble the bituanga tree whose fruit is fair but bitter, and whose roots alone are capable of giving nourishment.

We too easily connect the idea of charity with easy benevolence. We like the smiling expression, the kindly eye. These are the marks which appeal. What we forget is that they are marks only, and that the reality will cost us more than the labour of cultivating the smiling face and the kindly eye.

Charity does not exist to make us good mixers but to make us good Christians. From the supernatural point of view it matters little whether or not we are gregarious by nature; the important thing is that we be charitable by grace.

Christian charity goes beyond considerations of obligation, just deserts, rights and responsibilities: it searches positively for the good to love and the suffering to relieve. The Samaritan asked no questions, made no conditions, refused to examine the possibilities of being tricked. If the love of God is the motive, there is no possibility of being tricked.

In his chapter about charity St Peter says that as every man has received grace he must 'minister the same one to another as good stewards of the manifold grace of God'. Grace is not given to us for private and exclusive use: it must be allowed in charity to circulate.

In Christ we enter into the family of the race at its highest point of pedigree. We share in the circulation of His blood. Yet we can become so artery-hardened that as members we contribute little to the flow of love and grace through the mystical body.

The Christian is of the Blood Royal: he inherits and he must transmit. Each Christian is responsible for this immediate link in the tradition of Christ. Every link a vital value in the chain. The sequence of Christ's gospel, and therefore of charity, does not allow of gaps, of breaks, of dangling ends that swing in the air and are out of charity.

If Christ's life is mine, and mine is His, there must be something which I can do for my fellow members of His Body. The least I can do, and the most, is to communicate charity.

'If any man minister' says St Peter, 'let him do it as of the power which God administers.' God is not honoured by a ministry founded upon human power. The only ministry that can honour God is the one that honours Him through Jesus Christ our Lord. Without grace the minister is nothing. With grace, that is with charity, the minister is the channel of infinite influence.

No wonder that charity covers a multitude of sins. The covering may be thought of not so much as a screen hiding the evil and atoning for it, but more as a lid forcing down the evil into the dustbin forbidding it to poison the air. Where charity exists there is no scope for sin. Charity diverts the energy, taking desire away from self and into the region of its proper expression.

Charity covers not only a multitude of sins but a multitude of sorrows—both in one's own soul and in the souls of others. So much of life is spent in suffering that if it is to be bearable at all it needs to be spent in company and not alone. To give out charity and to receive it creates a temperature in which we are not so likely to be frozen by sorrow or despair.

At least when living in charity we have not the supreme loneliness to fear. Not only is Christ with us but we have the additional support of His members. Our hearts are enlarged in charity so that we are able to bear the difficulties of life; they are no longer our own difficulties but His. We still dread partings and misunderstandings as much as ever, and we are still as sensitive to their pain, but we know that all these things are in the pattern of love and that they may not be evaded.

Vulnerable we must remain till the end—charity is not designed to make us immune from sword-thrusts, and is certainly not to be taken up as a suit of defensive armour—but our wounds do not fester any more. The charity that has entered into the bloodstream keeps the whole organism in health: there is no bitterness on which corruption can gain a hold. 'Charity is patient, is kind ... seeks not its own.' The charity of Christ is the only true wisdom: it is not only the whole law but is also the whole happiness of man.

COMMUNICATION OF GIFTS

WHAT is the use of influencing another if you have nothing but your own wretched self to communicate? It only means that there will be two of you where there was one before. But communicate Christ, and at once the influence is worth while. It means that there will be one of you in Christ where there were two before.

To impart Christ is the highest office of man and the

137

greatest blessedness. If to impart self gives gratification, to impart grace gives a peace and bliss which the world cannot appreciate. If men can find their happiness in giving happiness to others, they can find Christ in giving Christ to others.

The giving of Christ to others depends entirely upon living in Christ oneself. It is only by faith and love that one soul can influence another supernaturally, and the degree of the influence is measured by the depths of the faith and love. 'He who believes in Me, out of his belly shall flow rivers of living water.'

The soul in whom the Spirit dwells is a fountain of grace to the thirsty. It is the Spirit that gives life, not the fountain. The fountain is merely the means chosen by the Spirit: it is the channel of grace from the reservoir. Or, to change from the gospel to the psalms, it is not only that 'in Thy light we shall see light', but that with Thy light we are empowered to lighten the darkness of others.

Why, when you preach, are you so anxious to make *yourself* clear? Preach Christ and the people will understand you. Why, when you write, do you worry about who will read what you write and whether you will be remembered as a writer when you are dead? Why, when you hear confessions, does the thought of what impression you are making on your penitent make any difference to the kind of advice you give and the way you give it?

It is right that when a man gives himself to God he should feel a great longing to give others to God as well, and that he should long to give God to them. He finds himself filled with a sense of mission: he is on fire.

If this soul examines the cause of this zeal he will realize, unless he is either very vain or a great idiot, that the sense of mission is a grace and that the fire is the fire of the Spirit.

It is not on account of any excellence of his that a man cares about the spiritual welfare of others; it is because God has set him in this direction. 'This is God's doing' says St Paul to the Corinthians, 'it is He who, through Christ, has reconciled us to Himself and allowed us to minister this reconciliation of His to others. Yes, God was in Christ reconciling the world to Himself, establishing in our hearts His message of reconciliation.'

Once set in the direction of ministering God's word to souls, the man of God goes ahead with Christ's blessing upon him. It is no merit of his that he preaches the gospel; woe unto him if he preach not the gospel. But he has to be sure that this is really what God wants. And, being sure, must take the trouble to train himself for the work.

'How shall they preach unless they be sent?' Yet there are some who run up the pulpit steps two at a time in their willingness to hear their own voices. 'Do not be too eager, brethren, to impart instruction to others' says St James; 'be sure that if we do we shall be called to account all the more strictly.' So long as we preach Christ, and in the spirit of Christ, we need not fear the responsibility. But how many of us preach Christ, the whole Christ, and nothing but Christ?

Nor is this matter of influencing others confined to the pulpit and the confessional. The most lasting influence, as well as the one that goes deepest, is the influence exercised by one soul upon another. So direct is this communication, so intimate a mode of expression, that self in one form or another is an inevitable element in the imparting of Christ. All the more reason that the self conveyed is the self which is becoming increasingly identified with Christ.

In order to influence another person we have to have understanding of that other person. There has to be sympathy before there can be communication. We are not likely to present much of Christ to those whose mental attitude is unintelligible to us or inexcusable. Our first duty, then, is to look for something about the other person that strikes a familiar note. The affinity may be to ourselves, but it must be to our identified selves. Thus, more importantly, it must be a joint affinity to Christ. The relationship which is based on anything other than a joint affinity to Christ is, supernaturally, to no purpose.

For mutual influence to produce spiritual good there has to be mutual receptivity: the one influenced must be ready to accept, and, having received, make return. *Quidquid recipitur est in recipiente secundum modum recipientis.*[1] If the recipient limits his capacity to benefit, nothing in the world—however good the thing given or however earnest the desire of the giver —can increase the good received. The man who expects the kingdom of God to be no bigger than a threepenny bit receives the kingdom of God as a threepenny bit. The sheer grace of God may widen him; nothing else will.

We do not influence weak characters: weak characters are influenced all over again by the next man to come along. You cannot carve a statue out of cotton wool. Nor, until they are humbled, can we influence vain characters. You cannot rule a straight line with the spring of a watch. The people whom we can influence are strong characters and characters who recognize the pride that is self. But if we work with Christ and for Christ, it may be that He will use us to bring to Him weak characters whom He will make strong, and vain characters whom He will make humble.

All human relationship must rely, inevitably, upon forms and symbols. Without some sort of mode of expression, human communication is impossible: there has to be a language or a sign if thought is to be conveyed from one mind to another. There has to be something outward.

Leaving out the question of grace for a moment, not even Socrates could have made himself felt had he never spoken a word, written a line, appeared before men. For personality to attract, there have to be terms. Before you can hang upon a man's thought or weigh his character, you have to hang upon his words and weigh his acts.

Not until the inward is expressed outwardly can the answering potency be awakened. There has to be a picture to see if the artist's inspiration is to be followed, a song if the poet is to share his emotion. And it is the same in the relationship of religion: 'The invisible things of God are clearly seen, being understood by the things that are made; so that they are inexcusable that have not glorified Him as God.'

[1] 'Whatever is received is received according to the disposition of the recipient.'

For the transmission of vitality from one human being to another there has to be life in each. If there is no responding vitality from the weaker member, the stronger member's vitality serves no purpose. It is no good giving a blood-transfusion to a corpse.

When one man influences another he does not impose character, he generates it. He picks up whatever is already there and breathes a new spirit into it, imparts an ideal, opens new ways. Medicine does not give health, it stimulates it. Education does not induce but educe. Religious life does not make the love of God; it stimulates the love of God that it finds.

Just as we receive Christ in proportion to our love, so we impart Christ in proportion to our love. But in the imparting there is this difference—that there must be love to receive love. 'The charity of God is poured forth in our hearts'—in our own hearts, and from us to other people—'by His Spirit dwelling in us.'

If His Spirit dwells in us, the influence which we exercise is spiritual. But there must be no nonsense about this: we must be subdued to the life of the spirit, not occasionally practised in it.

The more truly spiritual the influence, the less there may be to show for it. It is easy enough to make a quick superficial impression, but we are not talking about quick superficial impressions. The communication of the spirit is not a sudden action. Grafting takes time.

When we try to impart Christ sincerely, when we make serious efforts to keep our own personalities in the background, we are often saddened by the evidence of our failure. Is not this precisely because we *are* working in the spirit? If the whole of our effort were outward, we might be granted outward success, but because we are in labour until Christ be formed in us and we in Him—and because we are trying to reproduce exactly this operation in the souls of others—the result is hidden.

Why, we ask ourselves, is Christ's influence so marked in the case of the apostles and so unmarked in the case of ourselves? He who was so vividly present to His friends is so distressingly absent to me. Is this because I am a sinner, because I am not really trying? It may well be so, but more likely it is because of what we have seen above—namely that the apostles were admitted to one form of knowledge of Christ and that we are admitted to another. To them was granted an immediate experience of Christ, to us the experience comes through grace and by faith.

Whatever the form that Christ takes, the duty of the soul is to respond to that. Where the apostles shaped their lives round Christ and the knowledge which their direct appreciation gave them, we who come after shape our lives round Christ and the knowledge which our faith gives us. For us, no less than for the apostles, the Incarnation makes the Christ-life liveable. Where the apostles followed the concrete example, we have to follow the same example but by a different way.

'If I go not, the Paraclete will not come to you'—we have no cause to resent the disposition by which we grope towards Christ in spirit while the apostles had only to ask Him questions and would receive their answers. The influence then was by means of outward symbols: the influence now is by inward symbols. For those who have come after Christ's death there is only this one work: to form Christ by faith in their hearts.

Christ once formed by faith in our hearts, we shall inevitably impart the Incarnation. Then will mutual influence have nothing of danger in it. Then will His purpose be realized in our works, then will His love flow out from the tips of our fingers, then will His light shine from this beacon of rubbish which is ourselves.

So it is idle to worry about the effect we are producing on souls: we have not been asked to produce effects on them—God must be left to do that—but to serve them. All we have to consider is the effect His influence is having upon us—whether or not we are yielding completely to the impact of His character upon ours. My good impression upon the world counts for nothing, nothing at all; what matters is His impression upon me, and upon souls.

'Not changing nature but perfecting the will' says St John

142

Chrysostom of the Holy Spirit's work in the soul; 'finding a publican and producing an evangelist, finding a persecutor and producing an apostle, finding a thief and leading him into paradise, finding a harlot and putting her on an equality with virgins.' This is influence. No other kind is worth anything.

SIN

IF we had any idea of the effect which sin has upon our mortal natures we would never sin again. If we had any idea of the effect which sin has upon our immortal souls we would never sin again. So say the authorities; and they speak truly. Yet, knowing quite a lot about the effects of sin, we still go on sinning.

We talk about people being self-possessed, and we know from the psalmist that 'my soul is in my hands always', yet the fact remains that we are surprised again and again into sin. We are responsible and irresponsible at the same time. We have not the presence of mind to let reason hold its own against passion, and we have not the absence of mind which would excuse us from guilt.

All the time we are called to the heights, all the time we are capable of sinking to the depths. 'Why is it that Thou wilt make so noble a thing of man?' asks Job. 'Never a day dawns but Thou wilt surprise him at his post; never a moment when Thou art not making proof of him.'

Our every waking hour is spent in choosing, deciding, weighing the relative claims of virtue and vice, good and evil, God and greed. Our lives are lived out in a continuous movement, in a flux that becomes set only at the moment of death. Morally and spiritually we are forever swimming with or against the current.

Before, during, and after making up our minds about anything there are innumerable alternatives which we could take, could be taking, could have taken. The action which in effect we have decided upon is the result of a process, sometimes conscious and sometimes not, of mental balancing. 'What do I get out of this' is the question the soul asks itself, 'and is it worth it?' Whether the speculation takes an instant or a week, whether the evidence is fairly sifted or is dismissed by an imperious emotion before it ever appears before the bar of reason, the matching of desire against desire is the whole business of temptation and the whole business of trying to respond to grace.

When we sin we do not break something external to ourselves: the law that we break is something internal to ourselves, something intimate and personal, something designed by God with particular reference to our own specific sanctity. Infidelity to grace is not like smashing a window; it is more like choking a lung.

Each sin is in a sense the Fall over again. It is not merely the violation of a code; it is the loss of an innocence. Every temptation is Eve looking enviously at a tree; every sin is Adam taking a bite. We talk about our first parents representing us in the Fall, but we too re-present them. Actual sin is perilously close to original sin: the forbidden tree is still being rifled: we are still munching on its much-bitten fruit.

Though each sin is a new loss of grace, an isolated and unique disaster, it is not confined in its effect—any more than original sin was confined in its effect—to the immediate moment. Each sin, however out of keeping with the past record and however repented of afterwards, means a weakening of resistance to future temptation.

So frail is the natural barrier of character between innocence and guilt, between fidelity and infidelity, that the least departure from grace wears it thinner. Repeated sin rubs against the will, teasing it till it gives consent to lighter and lighter temptation. Temptation, returning over and over again to the same weakened spot, meets eventually with so little resistance that the soul is virtually defenceless, preferring to let things take their course, whatever the consequences, rather than to go on fighting and possess peace of conscience.

But it works both ways: each act of resistance to temptation gives new vitality to the will. Every response to grace makes further response easier, every act of love is a contribution to the pattern of love which is at the same time in a constant process of development and under constant threat of destruction.

We are not conditioned by the past, but the past cannot leave us uninfluenced. Whether it is the forbidden fruit or the fruit of the true vine, the taste remains.

Our souls at the close of our lives are what we have made of the temptations and graces which have been shaping us. Experience is our education for good or ill; experience is not a fleeting instruction to which we may or may not be paying attention.

This means that what we choose to do to-day is, on the balance and apart from miraculous intervention, of a piece with what we have been choosing to do all our lives. The people we are at this moment, and therefore the people we shall be when we come to die, are the normal ones. Not necessarily the most true, but inevitably the most normal. They are those for whom we are responsible: they are those whom we have chosen to call ourselves.

This person whom I think of as myself here and now, to-day, is the one whom I have been building up since I was a child. I have been tending towards my present self. My free decisions have been adding to me or taking away; my experience has been used, whether to make a mask or to make reality, to make me. I am my own norm. And what if that norm is false?

If I have spent my whole life plastering my face with make-up and moulding a figure in wax, if I have never come out into the light but shuffled about in the shadows where my sins and disguises seemed to stand a better chance, I shall look all the worse when the Sun of Justice shines full upon me on the day of judgment. The make-up will run and the wax will melt, and I shall be exposed.

Memory, as we possess it in this life, is kind to sin. Except in the case of those spasms of remorse and fear which come to us at intervals, time has a way of softening the edges of our failure. We look back and wonder why we were so foolish or so indiscreet or so irresponsible; we seldom look back and wonder at the criminal neglect of grace, at the hideous malice, at the filthy greed.

But at the judgment we shall be given more accurate memories with which to assess our responsibility. Then we shall know exactly how far we have repented and how far we have clung to our sin, how far we have deceived ourselves and others, how far we have fallen below the level to which grace was calling us *and to which we knew that grace was calling us.*

Then shall we be faced with the image of our two selves: the self that we have turned ourselves out to be, and the self that was in the mind of God when He created us. Then will the two selves merge into one, and at last we shall see ourselves as God sees us. And this may be the greatest shock of all.

But here again it works both ways. If the evil is to stand out to condemn us, may we not hope that there will be some good that will stand out to recommend us? Just as in this life we are constantly experiencing the wholly gratuitous lavishness of God's mercy, may we not trust that the same sort of thing will happen when we are tried for our lives in eternity?

So often in the past we have watched a crust harden over our souls and done nothing about it. Then God, seeing perhaps a movement of goodwill in our hearts, or possibly even seeing nothing there at all but an empty space which He wants to see filled with love, takes the initiative and breaks the shell. On the day of judgment, before sentence is passed, there will be evidence enough to damn our souls for ever. But perhaps by that time the outer cover of our souls will be lying in pieces, and the good which He has conjured out of us at the last moment of our mortal lives—the good which He has Himself placed there to conjure up—will be witness in our favour.

When the Father summons the soul to take the place prepared in heaven, it will not be because of any beauty which the soul has managed to design for itself. It will be because of the Son whom the Father sees reflected there. The indwelling will

146

then be the whole-dwelling, and there will be nothing to prevent the possession of the promise.

Not until my earthly nature, with its sins and evasions and self-deceptions, has been laid aside can I begin to live to full capacity. It is as if, while I am still in this world, I am forever pressing against the covering which holds me captive to human conditions *and at the same time* drawing closer the very folds that cover me: I long for escape into the new element which I know to be true, while at the same time I long for the protection of the old element which I know to be false.

Not till the earthenware vessels in the hands of Gedeon's men were broken did the light which was to bring them victory shine.

SELF

AVOIDING sin is difficult enough; the heartbreaking thing is trying to avoid self. Sin does not enter into everything that one does; sin can as a rule be recognized; sin gives scope for repentance and the determination to avoid the occasion. Self on the other hand is inescapable, cannot always be seen as self, is not something about which one normally feels remorse or can take practical steps to conquer.

However dull one knows oneself to be, however prosaic one's record from infancy onwards, however commonplace one's occupation and achievement, the one, central, pivotal, vital interest which never fails is oneself.

Are the saints self-centred to this extent? Did our Lady consider her own advantage from morning till night? Was Christ preoccupied with His own importance? The thought of such possibilities is almost irreverence. The answer then is clear: the self that is wholly subdued to grace is no drag upon the spirit, but rather the reverse. It is the self that acts according to nature, that lives in its own right, that seeks a recognition from the world and from its twin self which is endeavouring

147

to identify its whole being with Christ—this is the self that has to be brought into the open and denied.

Even when we are absorbed in the work which God has given us to do—so absorbed that we have no time to worry about its success or failure—we know at the back of our minds that it is *we* who are working. The work is going out from *our* hands. The action is being steered by *us* and by nobody else. Self and not God.

Even when we are praying on our knees and there is nobody watching us to see how spiritual we are, we have the comforting thought recurring constantly to our minds that we are doing something virtuous. We know that all mankind should be giving worship to God, and we take pleasure in the idea that we are among the number who do. Self and not God. Christ did not pray like this. The saints do not pray like this.

Even when we are being kind to people in the name of the gospel—perhaps the more so when in the name of the gospel —we are aware of many motives other than that of charity. We want to be thought kind, we want to *feel* kind, we want the rewards of kindness. Self and not God. The charity of the saints is something better than this.

When we are fasting, when we are keeping custody of the eyes, when we are exercising ourselves in even the humblest mortifications, self is there too—preening away and striking attitudes. It is strange that a man cannot deny himself without trying to gratify himself. Curious that self can be found in the sacrifice of self.

If all this is true of the way in which human beings love God, it is equally true of the way in which human beings love one another. You might think that true love on earth would be proof, if anything was, against selfishness. But not at all. The man who is truly and happily in love can be as self-regarding as the man who is truly and happily following a religious vocation.

A lover may be ready to make every sort of sacrifice for the beloved, but the person whom he sees in his mind's eye is himself. He sees the beloved as a figure at his side.

A lover may suppress in himself the least consent to jealousy, but if he is honest he will know that what he wants above everything in the world is the exclusive possession of the beloved.

A lover may give the greatest thing he has to the beloved—namely freedom, which is what God gives to us in the name of love—but threaded through this generosity is the bitter-sweet selfish pain of knowing exactly what it costs to do so.

So it would seem that the lover, more than another, has reason to expose his self-deceptions. Love is never more blinding than when it professes to look love in the face.

For as long as we see those whom we love only as they touch our own natures, adjusted to our own personalities, so long will they be to us mere adaptations of ourselves. In order to reach them as they are in themselves and in the sight of God, we have to leave ourselves out of all account and make their happiness and holiness our aim. *Et nos debemus pro fratribus animas ponere.*[1]

'Of course' you will say, 'but how? If a man cannot work, pray, meet people, fall in love—still less do penance, give alms, preach and practise the works of mercy—without interpreting everything according to his own individuality, what is to be done? Even the gospel does not provide a formula for excluding self from our approach to life.'

It is not so much a matter of excluding self as directing self. In the measure that we pray and look for Christ we bypass the claims of self. Our minds are finite, and we cannot attend wholly to Christ without forgetting self. Let go of Christ and at once we fall back into self-pity and self-examination and self-dramatization.

Allow self the least consideration and we think about nothing but ourselves, we talk about nothing but ourselves, we come to be nothing but the most smothering bores.

So long as we project ourselves upon the screen of our own lives, let alone upon the screen of other people's lives, we see everything out of focus. We stare at ourselves, and the

[1] 'And we should lay down our lives for our friends.'

image—the image of God which we are meant to be—becomes blurred. If our focus of vision were trained upon God, we would both see ourselves clearer and see others in their right relation to ourselves and to God.

If we gaze at ourselves instead of at God whom we reflect, we block out the most important feature to be seen. It is not that the screen is too small, or that our range of vision is not wide enough, or that God does not present Himself recognizably before us. It is because the only person I am interested in is myself.

The only solution, as it is the only solution for all our problems, is the right understanding of love. It is no solution to say 'I must not think about myself ... if I think about myself I shall only talk about myself, pouring out my troubles to people and demanding their sympathy.' Such a determination is a good practical help, but it touches only the surface. A more radical solution would be to say 'I must pray more, and try to shape my mind according to the mind of Christ. I must make His thought mine. Then there will be no room for selfish greed, self-pity, and the demand for recognition.'

If only we loved God more we should not have to concern ourselves about this gnawing ache within us which never ceases to clamour for sympathy, flattery, affection.

If only our prayer would teach us to love God for Himself and not for the satisfaction of loving Him, or for His gifts, we would be granted more light on how to handle self-interest. The light on our self-interest comes only when God sees that we are prepared to do something to correct it.

As a general rule God withholds His light from the soul who is not detached enough from self to do His will. He would rather have the soul in darkness and in good faith than in light and in possible bad faith.

Light is not given us for the sole purpose of seeing our own failings: it is given us primarily so that we may look more lovingly towards Him.

If we made it our whole business to face what we saw in the light of prayer, we would be holier and happier and have a far greater influence on others. Yet in the face of so obvious a truth we still fear to look at what the light shows us.

Self shrinks from seeing self, and in consequence misses the light which would show it far more than self.

What the soul needs to see is more of the love of God, more of God Himself. The fruit of light is love, and love is the fulfilment of desire.

Our attitude towards God, towards others, towards ourselves is wholly dependent upon our understanding and practice of love. If we think of God primarily as relating to our own happiness we shall never grasp the full significance of religion. If we think of others as primarily related to our own happiness we shall not even begin to grasp the significance of charity.

Not until self is surrendered to God can grace so flood the soul as to possess it utterly. Only then will the soul's relationships be truly unselfish. The soul may still continue to see the weaknesses of its fallen nature—indeed will see them far more clearly than before—but will see them and not give in to them.

The under-the-surface workings of self will come into the light for condemnation, not for condoning. The soul will be so strengthened in the identification with Christ that whatever is outside Christ stands self-repudiated.

As in the case of human relationships, so in the case of divine relationship. The knowledge that another is fond of us, has an idealized concept of us, not only sublimates but ultimately excludes the baser qualities in our characters. If we are to respond to the other's love we have no room for the unpleasant side of ourselves: we rise above it, we forget it.

The knowledge that God loves me, is constantly thinking of me with affection, is concerned with my happiness and takes pleasure in my triumphs, is deeply and personally involved in my trials, must in the end invite so complete a surrender to His love that, as in the case of human response to human love, the baser elements are purified and turned to gold.

God has given Himself thus to me, and in the gift there is nothing of what we call 'self'. I can give myself to Him, and in

151

the gift I can revoke what we call self. More, I can elevate it. I can let Him assimilate my whole being into His so that the dregs of fallen humanity are turned towards His love and reconsecrated. Behold, He can make all things new.

RELIGIOUS LIFE

THE purpose of the religious life is to promote union with God. Whatever else it may do for the subject—or for the country, or for the particular religious order, or for the Church —if it fails to advance souls towards perfection, it has lost the main reason for its existence.

The religious life possesses all the means for the sanctification of its subjects. It is the channel of further grace to those who have been granted the initial grace of vocation. If subjects are not sanctified by living in religion under vows, it means either that they are not trying to sanctify themselves or that the particular form of religious life under which they are serving God is not trying to sanctify them.

Every failure in the religious life can be traced either to personal infidelity on the part of the subject to the religious ideal or to the general infidelity of the institution which is meant to represent the ideal.

Because the religious life exists for the sanctification of the subject and not the subject for the sanctification of the religious life, the responsibility of conveying grace to the subject is no less binding upon the religious life than the responsibility of responding to grace is binding upon the subject. In practice this means that those whose duty it is to shape and foster the spirit of their communities may not forget their office for a single instant.

There is nothing wanting to the ideal of the religious life: it aims at making the Christ-life imitable. The religious life proposes the practical unfolding of the gospel.

By obedience the subject is emptied—as Christ by His own

will was emptied, becoming obedient unto death—of the many forms of self considered in the foregoing section. If Christ was emptied of a self which was infinitely perfect in order to become an example of infinitely perfect obedience, we, in the subjection imposed by obedience, become perfect in the perfection which is His.

By poverty, chastity, unworldliness, regular observance, community life, recollection and the liturgy, souls in religion are drawn towards the transformation in grace which is the end of Christian man.

If we think of the religious vocation primarily as something which demands, we think of it incompletely and wrongly. Vocation is, as the very word states, the first move: it is the grace which is not only itself a gift but which carries with it the promise of an endless sequence of gifts.

The religious vocation is the more precise application of the words addressed to all Christians: 'You have not chosen Me, but I have chosen you.'

The religious vocation is the exhortation 'Be ye perfect as your heavenly Father is perfect' brought one step nearer.

The religious vocation is the practical answer to Christ's 'If thou wilt be perfect'—applied no less personally than in the case of the rich young man.

The religious vocation is the gift of peace and freedom and happiness to souls who are at the same time given the means to pay for these things. But if they refuse to pay for them, the gifts turn to dust in their hands.

Where the problem for the soul living in the world is how to bring observance into line with principle, the problem for the soul in religion is almost in a sense the reverse: it is how to relate the spiritual impulse with the existing regular observance.

If the letter does not quicken the spirit, it is apt to kill it. But the letter goes on. And what is to quicken the letter if the spirit is dead?

If observance is to be a living service and not a dead routine, it must be renewed in spirit every day. Like love and sanctity and humility, the service of God in religion knows no exchanges of motive power. The religious state that derives its momentum from nature is no religious state.

Lose sight of the supernatural and at once you have nothing to lean on but your own human strength. And who could live the religious life by the force of his character alone? It is difficult enough to lead the religious life by the power of grace: without the power of grace the life would not only do no good but would do positive harm.

No religious has ever done harm, either to his own soul or to another's, where he has relied wholly upon grace. The harm that religious have done is always due to independence of grace. It is not only passion, ambition, greed that break upon the smoothness of religion's record; it is as often the wrong sort of confidence.

If we trust in our fixed purpose, in the nobility of our nature, in our sense of propriety, in our blameless past or our ability to provide for the future, we are in danger. Sooner or later we shall be caught out. The only way to be faithful to our state as religious is to trust in nothing short of God.

The religious who is self-confident is ready to take risks. He feels so secure about his poverty (or his chastity, or his obedience, or whatever the particular religious virtue) that he interprets its application. He considers himself in possession of the essence, and so can dispense himself from the accidentals. As self-deception grows, and as the help of grace diminishes, he leans more and more upon weaker and weaker supports. Humanly speaking—and there is nothing but human data now to go upon—there is nothing to prevent his sinning against his state.

If it is folly to rely upon natural powers in the performing of a supernatural service, it is equally folly to rely upon external observance as a substitute for interior progress. The religious life is progressive or it is nothing. The religious life is interior or it is nothing.

External observance, unsupported by interior effort, may keep a man going in self-satisfaction for a time—he will be able

154

to point to nice little things like punctuality and custody of the eyes when his conscience reproaches his self-esteem—but he will not be happy for long. And it will be a sterile happiness that he enjoys, incapable of being shared and ignorant of the meaning of love and sacrifice.

To love external observance may be either a good thing or a bad thing. It depends entirely upon what such a love leads to. In itself religious observance has, without grace, no more value than any other fidelity to rule.

A man may like to follow a religious routine or a man may dislike it. It is not a question on which he will be required to give an account. There are saints who have felt no satisfaction whatever in fulfilling their obligations as religious; there are other saints who seem to have enjoyed their religious duties to the full. The determining quality for both kinds was not the pleasure they found in the service of God but the readiness they gave to the service of God.

We do not persevere in religious life because we love observance but because we love God. We do not keep our vows as religious because they suit us but because they suit God.

It is a mistake to judge religious according to whether they have or have not found happiness in their vocation. They have not come into religion to find happiness; they have come to find God.

It is a mistake to think of a religious vocation as providing a solution to a particular person's problem. Vocation has something better to do than to cure disorders. God gives vocations to souls so that they may come the most direct way to Him—and solve their own problems in the process.

It is a mistake to think of souls entering religion for the liturgy, for the peace, for this or that apostolic work, for the opportunity of study. God may draw souls by playing upon their attraction towards any of these things—there are different gates to the temple, different fountains to the spring—but unless such souls come into religion in order to serve Him they will find that those very attractions which led them towards God will be their greatest obstacles to finding Him.

To misread a signpost is not merely to do without information: it is to be diverted from the right direction.

To enter religion for the sake of the company you find there is as foolish as to take out naturalization papers on the strength of a travel poster. You enter from charity, not for companionship.

To enter religion because you admire a religious is as foolish as to wear summer clothes in winter because you enjoy the sun. The particular person whom you admire will die or be sent to another house of the order, and you will be left in your summer habit.

To enter religion in order to find leisure for literary work, or artistic work, or just to find an escape from the work you are doing in the world, is equally to enter backwards. In the Father's house there are many mansions, but you may not enter if all you want to do is to sit down in the chairs.

In order to live the religious life fruitfully you will have need of great faith. Not only must you try to give to it and forget about what you are gaining from it, but you must do without the satisfaction of seeing yourself making the gift.

You may have to stand by and see your hopes disappointed, your plans reversed, your values devalued, and your good intentions misunderstood. You may be let down, disedified, passed over; but none of this matters in the least. You have come into religion in order to love God, and the love of God is the only thing that counts. For the rest you must make acts of faith—loving so far as you can the instruments of your frustration.

FORESHORTENED SANCTITY

HOW is it that the monk or nun can miss the spirit of the order? How can the religious be excused for not being *this particular kind of religious*? How, after the vows have been taken, can there be doubt? Where, with the Rule in black and white, is the difficulty ? The answer is that if Christians can so easily miss the Christ-life, religious can just as easily miss the religious life.

Whether in religion or in the world, the soul must propose to itself 'the most excellent knowledge of Christ'. He who sees Christ sees also the Father, and this is eternal life to know the Father and Jesus Christ whom He has sent. Monasteries and convents are founded for no other reason than to teach precisely this knowledge. In the world it is less easy to learn the finer points of the wisdom of Christ, but it is possible enough. And grace makes it more than possible enough.

The knowledge, once acquired, can do one of two things: it can develop until it fills the whole horizon, bringing life and light and strength and hope and love. Or it can lie dead in the mind, like a precious stone at the bottom of a lake.

Knowledge, when stirring the will to action, starts the pendulum swinging—intellect and desire mutually assisting one another and keeping time. Knowledge, when sterile, puffeth up. This second knowledge (which is really the same knowledge as the other but received by a different disposition) has nothing to say to the will. So the pendulum does not even begin to swing.

An abstract, transcendental, theoretical religion is an anomaly. Reason may not be restricted to itself. The exercise of the intellect, even when operating on Christian truth, can be morally fruitless. Whatever Aristotle may say about the highest happiness being found in mental speculation and the acquisition of knowledge, thought as such has no supernatural value. But once it is harnessed to action the whole scene changes.

To enjoy the delights of theological thought is no more meritorious than to enjoy the delights of anything else. It responds to a taste—like jam. People imagine that because they are interested in dogma, or the liturgy, or ecclesiastical art, or church ceremonial, they are on that account spiritually superior to those who are interested in the theatre or growing mushrooms. But since natural interest is awakened only by natural stimuli, it cannot greatly matter—from the super-natural point of view, and granted that the outward stimulus is not evil in itself—what it is that rouses enthusiasm. It is neither the stimulant nor the interest that matters in the spiritual life, but the spiritual and moral effect that is produced.

To appreciate intellectually and not to translate into terms of actuality would be to leave the absolutely important at the level of the relatively important.

The practical consequences of thought have to be looked at as carefully as the thought itself. The Christian soul, and more especially the contemplative Christian soul, must know all about the relation between thought and conduct. That is why faith and morals always go together.

Faith, slightly misunderstood, can overlook morals. The false mystic, living by an obscure faith of his own, feels himself to be above the elementary laws of Christian behaviour. He thinks he is directed immediately by the Holy Spirit who can transcend His own law.

Morals in the same way, slightly misunderstood, can be intolerant of the yoke of faith. The false moralist, living by the dead code of good behaviourism, will find himself just as much at the mercy of temptation as the false mystic. In the last analysis it is temptation, not theory, that proves the quality of a man who on paper may be orthodox enough.

For the true service of God, a man must be able to get himself into a harmony of parts, must find his intellectual convictions and his canons of practical conduct so squared off that there are no inconsistencies or contradictions.

The Christian soul who is seriously following the grace of his prayer should find himself increasingly at one within himself. He should be establishing an ordered relationship not only between his soul and God but also between himself and God's creatures, between his interior attraction and his external obligation.

That spirituality is false which sacrifices harmony to eccentricity. Wherever there is a bulge, there is a corresponding hollow. In the case of souls who might so nearly be saints but

158

are not, the failure is almost always due to a preoccupation with one aspect of sanctity at the expense of the whole sanctity which is Christ's.

Arrested sanctity in souls is seldom due to their not going far enough all along the line; it is more often due to their going too far all along one line.

Sanctity means not only seeing things in their relation to God and one another, but so balancing their relative importance as to act according to grace and not according to nature.

The equilibrium of the saints, even though it may be disturbed by sudden infidelities immediately repented of, is something quite different from natural poise. Natural poise is the sheen of self-possession: supernatural serenity is the inevitable effect of being possessed by grace.

Sometimes we see in the conduct of the saints what appears to be an over-emphasis, a want of due order. This should not puzzle us when we realize that in the wider plan of God it has been necessary to correct a particular abuse or to shine the light upon a particular need.

Only in the lives of those who are not quite saints do we see the discrepancies which neither correct what is wrong nor draw attention to what is right. Here the stress is not upon the expression of God's will but upon the exhibition of personality.

The would-be saint may cause a great stir, attract a reputable following, act with admirable discretion and be guilty of no excesses that anyone could reasonably take exception to, but if he is running a work of his own, no work that he does can last.

The saint whose whole existence is the sanctity of Christ may cause no sort of stir whatever, may boast of no disciples, may be tactless, incompetent, foolish according to educational standards, but if he is bent upon furthering God's interests in preference to his own—as he must do if he lives in the spirit of Christ—his work for the world will be beyond computation.

What then are the signs by which we may recognize sanctity when we see it ? How are we to distinguish true from false? If even the fruits of man's work may be mistaken, is there no way of judging the spirit that prompts the work?

'Charity seeks not her own.' Of all the indications, this is probably the surest. Just as the devil can masquerade as an angel of light, so false humility can pass itself off as true, false zeal as true, false patience as true ... and so on. There exists also a false charity, as there exists a false virtue of every sort, but it will show itself up eventually in a self-seeking which may not be disguised.

To the soul who professes to be seriously searching after Christ there is only one unhappiness—the unhappiness of having missed Him.

The soul who falls short of sanctity, however faithfully the acts of sanctity are imitated, falls short in the measure that the challenge of true charity is evaded. Charity and self cannot share the possession of the soul.

Charity can weaken self, and self can weaken charity. The issue of sanctity is decided upon which of the two gains the upper hand.

THE LIGHT OF PRAYER

FOR most of us it is only by prayer that we can discover the hidden obstacles to our perfection. The obstacles are nearly all of our own making, but this does not prevent us from being blind to them.

When other people tell us our faults, showing us how incompatible they are with the ideal which we have set ourselves to follow, we do not believe them. We think they have not seen deeply enough into our natures and so have mistaken our intentions. Our friends do not realize how noble we are ... and we go on our way.

When we read books which exactly describe our state, exploding our self-deceptions and pointing to a more complete surrender of self as the only remedy, we say that these books are necessarily laying down a general doctrine. They cannot be expected to legislate for the particular case.

When we listen to advice in the confessional, hearing things about ourselves which we dimly suspect to be true, we say 'He knows me only from what he sees of me here ... it is my background that makes all the difference.'

But our prayer does not let us escape like this. Prayer leaves us no excuse. The light shines into the remotest corners of the soul, exposing the most secret hypocrisies and leaving not a shred of self-congratulation anywhere.

When the last illusion about ourselves has been lit up and shown to be hollow, a new instrument is brought to bear. It is as if the red tip of the cauterizing needle sears the soul, burning away the corrupt matter in an action which causes infinite disgust. The surface writhes and sizzles while the smoke goes up.

It is now that we taste humility for perhaps the first time; hitherto we have merely meditated upon it. Humility is being branded in. We see that it is here a question of choosing between humility and despair, and the grace which comes of our awakening steers us towards humility: we throw ourselves upon God's mercy, knowing that we have nothing of our own that can save us.

Our memory shows us a list of half-forgotten infidelities; our imagination builds up a lurid picture of our guilt. Reason reproaches us for having so consistently acted independently of its light; the will has no explanation to offer for the way in which we have misused true liberty and followed the attraction of our lower nature.

In the light which this prayer brings us—in this revelation—we see how self-interest has tarnished what we had thought were our most golden acts. We wonder if we have ever done a single thing from a pure motive; and even if we have started to do something for the love of God, have we not before very long made shabby concessions to the love of self?

It is possible to shut out this light and to pray along lines which have no such searching effects. But what good will discursive prayer be to us and to the greater glory of God if we fall back upon it in flight from our own good and from the greater glory of God?

Jacob wrestled with an angel and it did him no good at all. Balaam denied the light of God and it caused him endless trouble later on. Jonas lived to regret his flight from the message of the Lord. We gain nothing from hiding from the face of God and from the sight of our own misery.

To turn away from light does not simply mean a return to ignorance. It does not simply mean a return to darkness. It is not strictly a return at all: it puts us in a new condition—a condition of more or less bad conscience, more or less bad faith.

The lights that we fail to follow up are not merely wasted here and now; they amount to a darkness which renders us less able to benefit by them if God should happen to offer them to us again.

Though we are never compelled to receive God's graces, the deliberate rejection of a grace has so lowering an effect upon our response to grace that it may well spread to a more general neglect.

We may tell ourselves that we are not fleeing from the light of God, and that we are only plucking up our courage to turn round and face it. 'I want God, but I am playing for time ... as soon as I have recovered from the shock of seeing myself so clearly I will come back for more.' But what is to guarantee that we shall come back for more?

The glare is harder to face each time. Each time it gets easier to run away and hide. We can become more used to running away than to looking towards the light. So of course in the end God lets that kind of light go out. The soul may be prepared to waste light, but God is not.

No member of a household whose responsibility it is to light the rooms of the house at a certain hour will keep up the practice indefinitely if those for whose benefit the arrangement was made are habitually entertaining themselves at that time elsewhere.

Just as our senses very quickly adjust themselves to particular pressures that are constant or recurring, so our interior faculties can accustom themselves to vibrations of the spirit. A man whose work is at first interrupted by the sound of trains can soon work undisturbed: it is not that he cannot hear the trains, but that he does not notice them.

A dealer can get so used to looking at pictures good and bad, at statues and works of decoration, that the critical faculty which has been given to him for the appreciation of beauty no longer operates. It is not that he cannot distinguish between true and false, but that he no longer bothers to.

Appreciation of light and of truth is, like the appreciation of external excellence, an interior quality. So if, by the rejection of light and truth, we choose to follow our own will instead of answering an invitation from God—if for example we neglect the impulse which prompts us to read more deeply or pray more often or go out to others more generously or mortify ourselves more thoroughly—we do not merely turn down something outside ourselves but actually produce a blunting effect upon something inside ourselves. Our sensibility to invitation, let alone the invitation itself, is slighted.

It is human nature to de-value what it has abused, and it is common experience to find souls belittling the interior life which once they very much wanted to pursue. God does not lessen His appeal unless we first lessen the readiness of our acceptance. And where we do lessen the readiness of our acceptance we tend, in self-defence, to discredit the true nature of what we have rejected. 'It was only a very uncertain light ... one is not bound to follow these little inspirations ... it was a question not of sin but of imperfection ... one cannot be expected to live at the level of sanctity all the time.'

If we could be sure that a rejected grace would turn out to be a lasting reproach, repeatedly reminding us of our folly and stirring us to make up with love for what we have lost with our laziness, we would at least have a constant light to go by. But we become just as conditioned to the reproaches of our conscience as we become conditioned to the call of grace: indeed they are the same voice. And where we deny the voice we walk in darkness.

Wanting only our own will, we forgo the will of God. Forgoing the will of God, we forgo the one thing which we wanted when we decided to follow our own will.

It is not only a paradox that in preferring self we impoverish ourselves; it is not only a punishment for our greed. It is the supreme calamity of a wasted freedom. What is even sadder is that, having rejected the light and having groped in the darkness, we shrink from seeing more clearly.

For as long as we can pray 'Lord that I may see' we are safe: it means that, however little or however much we know about ourselves, we have some sort of intention of doing God's will rather than our own. But if in our wretchedness we are afraid of the light, knowing that we may have to see more than we bargained for, we are in danger of stopping on in our darkness. It is thus that men can love darkness better than the light.

THE DEMAND OF PRAYER

INTERIOR prayer is nothing more nor less than the making actual, under the operation of the Holy Spirit, of certain powers received by the soul at baptism and otherwise lying latent. The grace of contemplation enables the soul to use these powers, more or less at will, in the direct praise of God.

It is only accidentally, and considered numerically, that contemplatives are the exceptions rather than the rule. The grace of contemplation is not for the privileged few but for the privileged many: it is designed in the Providence of God to be the outcome of the pursuit of holiness.

Though freely given by God, the grace of contemplation is normally attainable by those who seriously try to merit it. 'Merit' is here an unfortunate word, suggesting rights rather than privileges, but in the sense that the soul may confidently expect a proffered grace by positively and negatively disposing himself to receive it, the word may serve.

Positively the soul is disposed towards contemplation by the effort to practise the virtues, to love God inside the time of prayer and out, to look for the will of God in all things. Negatively the soul is disposed towards contemplation by avoiding occasions of distraction, by mortifying the senses, by not clinging to any of the forms of discursive prayer when interiorly drawn to a more simple exercise of attention or recollection.

For so long as we trust in any industry of ours to win us contemplation we are denied contemplation. This is not so much a punishment for our pride as a necessary consequence of our blindness.

Before contemplation can come in to flood the soul and fill it (though secretly and obscurely) with love, the purifying process which we have been examining in the foregoing pages must rid it of both illusion and creatures.

'The caverns of the soul's powers are not conscious of their extreme emptiness' says St John of the Cross, 'when they are not purified and cleansed from all affection to created things. Every trifle that enters them is enough to perplex them, to render them insensible to their loss and unable to recognize the infinite good which is wanting, or of their own capacity for it.'

The demands of the interior life are, therefore, considerable. Nothing may be snatched at before the time for its receiving, nothing may be clung to at the moment of its withdrawing. It is a question of tempering the appetite to the divine need, and this may take a lifetime and require much grace. But it may also take scarcely any time at all, and in this case there will have to be a still more powerful influx of grace.

When the 'caverns of the soul' which St John of the Cross writes about are emptied of affection to creatures—and this is done in the active and passive night of sense—there is a sense of loss which is almost unbearable. The soul has nothing of its old satisfaction to fall back upon, and it is incapable as yet of appreciating whatever light is coming to it.

The demand now is one of faith. The soul must be ready to put up with the sense of interior emptiness for as long as God may want; there must be no forcing of the imagination into the work of meditation. To look for sweetness when the time of sweetness is over—and the period of sensible devotion is not normally prolonged—is to delay the action of grace. Contemplation cannot come to the soul that is stirring itself into an artificial fervour.

As soon as the soul is adapted to the gift—that is to say when love is ready to meet love—the grace of contemplative knowledge and vision is granted, and a new life is begun. Then it is that the soul can turn round on itself and see that the whole process has been the work of God: He has prepared, emptied, and now freely filled the soul with light.

Once the soul has begun to respond to the infused light of contemplation the desire to go back to meditation abruptly stops. The whole desire is now directed towards the more direct love of God: the appetites of the soul have no other satisfaction than that of resting quietly in loving attention upon God.

The soul does not have, for safety sake, to busy itself any longer with discursive processes. All it has to do is to lean towards the love which is its whole life and happiness. The prayer exercise is by no means wholly passive—as it would be if the soul yielded to a pleasurable blank—but is active at a new and different level.

Contemplation expresses itself in actively receiving. If it ceased to act it would cease to love, and to love is the one constant all-embracing desire of the soul.

St John of the Cross says of the soul receiving the knowledge of contemplation that it must be like the air which the sun warms and purifies in proportion to its calmness and purity. Anxiety disturbs the calm, attachment disturbs the purity. To worry about one's spiritual state, questioning the validity of the action of grace, would here be as damaging as to look for pleasure in either prayer or people.

It is no easy thing to stifle the doubts which rise up in the mind and clamour for settlement. 'How am I to know that my prayer is not plain idleness? Has not the change from active prayer to contemplation been nothing but delusion?' The act of faith which answers these questions is precisely the demand which is made of the soul in the prayer of contemplation.

That the prayer outlined above is not an easy way out, not the deception practised by those who cannot be troubled to meditate, is shown by the accounts which are given of it by the souls whose witness is most to be respected. If there were anything wrong about the prayer of waiting upon God in simple regard, the saints would not have gone on from the practice of it to the higher states which were theirs later on. A deluded prayer would have brought their progress to a halt.

To rest in God, to sit still in His presence without saying anything, to maintain a receptive rather than a contributive attitude towards Him—this does not mean doing nothing at all. It means doing nothing of what the soul has been used to doing before—namely reasoning and picturing, and stirring the sensitive faculties.

While the soul is practising the prayer of simple regard there is a constant, though verbally unformulated, desire to love God. There is the positive, and even reiterated, surrender of self. There is the implicit, but no less real because not framed in so many words, petition that God may come and unite the soul with Himself.

Far from ministering to laziness and self-satisfaction, such a prayer is both stimulating and humiliating. It reveals to the soul, in a way which books and sermons can never do, the need to serve God with all one's soul and strength; it fills the soul at the same time with a knowledge of its utter worthlessness. Painfully aware of insufficiency, tempted to despair of ever being able to respond to the calls of grace, overwhelmed by the discovery of God's love and solicitude and mercy, the soul that practises this prayer is not greatly inclined to laziness. Nor is vanity the present obstacle.

The demand of faith and perseverance is the greatest demand that can be made of the soul at any stage of the spiritual life: it *is* the spiritual life. It is in this early part of contemplation that the qualities most needed in the more advanced states are tested.

167

The question before the soul at its initiation into the ways of the spirit is simply whether or not to surrender absolutely, and to stay so surrendered for the rest of one's life. The soul knows that it is physically possible to go back, that it is God's will that it should go forward, that there will always be the help of grace to depend upon. The choice has been made by God; it is now for the soul to choose.

The beginning of contemplation, then, is an obscure, but a very deep and real, hunger for God. It differs from earlier spiritual hungers in that it wants neither the gifts of God nor anything else besides God.

Unsatisfying though this prayer must necessarily be—because God does not reveal Himself to the faculties which cry out for Him—the soul asks for nothing more than to stop on before God in loving desire. The whole of its being is felt to go into the desire for God: the senses may clamour but they count for nothing.

This is not to say that superficial appetites are wholly under control; it is to say that even while they are escaping control there is the solid conviction in the soul that God alone can satisfy its desire.

Especially strong is this impression of God as the sole, absolute, and exclusive object of the soul's affective powers during the actual time of prayer. It can then amount to a positive ache and even agony. It is the sickness of love—yearning stretched out from emptiness.

The greatest part of the pain is caused not by feeling denied of the object desired, but by feeling inadequate to the implications of the desire. The soul—having learned at least this much about love, that it is essentially self-giving—is dismayed to the depths by the thought of wanting so much and giving so little.

The soul is on fire to possess God and cannot possess Him; it is on fire to give, but finds it has nothing to offer.

While the powers of the soul feel nothing but frustration they are in fact being secretly satisfied. What is more, they are being drawn into unity and into union. The desire to be still with God in solitude is evidence that already, and without its knowing it, the soul is finding itself in its proper object. 'If you had not already found Me, you would not now be looking for Me.'

What the soul has at this stage above all to bear in mind is that, left to its own judgment, it will misunderstand God's plan; its only chance is to leave the whole operation in His hands. The ordinary systems of measurements being not only useless but misleading, there is nothing the soul can do in the assessing of its progress.

The course now to be followed is, apparently, ridiculously simple: the practice of patient endurance and hope is the demand of the moment, and the soul's whole effort should be directed towards these particular aspects of its faith.

The quality of this interior endurance, this fidelity to a reason unseen and unproved, is of such a kind that it can bring the soul swiftly through the early darknesses of contemplation. Unquestioning and unanxious, the soul is beginning to practise the virtue which it shall most need later on.

The hope which is here required of the soul is not that which hopes in a solution—or in a miracle, or in any particular grace which will bring relief—but that which hopes quite simply in God.

These are the demands which prayer makes of the contemplative soul.

THE NIGHTS OF PRAYER

WE have seen that in order to become contemplative, the soul must not only release its hold on its closest and most intimate attachments but must also allow itself to be deprived of all its known standards of spiritual valuation. 'To possess the All, you must leave all'; to love God alone, you must live alone to God.

The process by which the soul attains to freedom alike from creatures and from material conceptions of God takes place in what spiritual writers call the Nights of Sense and Spirit. The first night purifies the lower faculties of the soul, the second purifies the higher.

In the two nights the soul is both prepared for the life of faith and settled in it. The nights are thus chosen by God to be the immediate cause and the remote effect of contemplation. Contemplation accordingly becomes the appropriate expression of the knowledge learned in the nights, while the knowledge in its turn is increased by the act of contemplation. Indeed they are not two operations but one, rising in a single ascent to God.

Not until the mind has experienced the darkness caused by the effort to apply natural intelligence to supernatural truth can supernatural intelligence properly come into play. Equipped with this purified faculty—purified by grace in the first of the nights—the soul perceives truth with what St John of the Cross calls 'luminous knowledge'.

Luminous apprehension of God is not to be understood as evident apprehension: luminous here means that the knowledge of God by the theological virtue of faith enters a new dimension—the material world of creatures is felt to be transparent, and the real world of God is felt to stand solid behind it.

If the knowledge of God became any clearer than this, the night would not be a night at all but a dawn. An essential feature of the night is that all apprehension of God is beyond explanation, and that the attempt to explain makes deeper the darkness. The light which comes in the night does not shine upon truth to light it up for the satisfaction of the soul: the light which comes in the night makes truth more important and desirable to the soul, but less self-evidently visible.

'The soul cannot enter into the night of itself' says St John of the Cross, 'because no one is able of his own strength to empty his heart of all desires so as to draw near unto God.' This first night, the night of sense, is a time of active and passive purification, and the darkness of it varies in degree according to the activity or quiescence of the soul's endurance.

The night is thus progressive, beginning with the soul's active co-operation in the work of detachment, going on to the second stage where God takes over the act of stripping the soul of its too human modes of apprehension, and finishing up with the infusion of light and knowledge.

During the whole of this night the sensitive part of the soul is darkened. (That is why it is called the night of sense.) The speculative reason has nothing which is not advanced by sense-experience to work upon, so is no help in bringing assurances of safety to the soul; the will, starved of a nourishment which normally comes to it from the imagination and the memory, is without sensible impulse; the emotions are, under the impact of a light which they are incapable of assimilating, in abeyance.

Throughout this night the soul is tempted to go back and work up a light of its own. It knows that it is free to try. It feels that the light which was enjoyed when practising meditation and discursive prayer would bring relief. Some souls do in fact go back, but those that do make little progress until they decide to start all over again and to aim at the heights.

Those who keep to the course of interior prayer and desolation must remember that they would not be keeping to it but for the sheer grace of God. They must not judge the less courageous, nor allow themselves to feel superior. The dividing line is very thin; the soul may stumble across it one way or the other. And often the soul is in such darkness that it does not know which way it has stumbled—forward or back.

Indeed the only sign now is whether or not there is, in the highest and coolest (and now perforce narrowest) region of the will, the desire to be united with God for His sake alone. This is a test which, even though all the other faculties are reduced to impotence, can be made to register.

It is precisely to this test that the night has been bringing the soul. The question which has to be freely decided upon by the responsible agent—namely the soul itself, whose responsibility survives its surrender—is: 'Am I ready to forgo all my own ideas and hopes, leaving everything in God's control, or do I identify my own happiness with something short of God?' If I submit myself to God and rest in His will, I have passed the test and have come to the dawn; if I rest in the hope of anything else at all, I have not passed the test and am still in the night.

So although it is not left to the soul to enter the night, it is left to the soul, through either its obstinacy or laziness or fear, to prolong it. God rewards only His own works, and the night that is induced by the soul belongs to the soul, and is its punishment.

The night that does not lead to surrender leads to entrenchment in self.

The night that does not lead to the luminous knowledge of God leads to an unenlightened preoccupation with creatures.

The night that does not lead to humility and charity leads to vanity and suspicion of others.

The night that does not lead to truth leads to fear of the truth and to an endless sequence of evasions and substitutions and impostures.

Though much of what has been said applies to the night of the spirit as well as to the night of sense, there are distinguishing features about the night of the spirit which have to be noted and allowed for.

The night of the spirit is not so much a purgation as a preparation. It disposes the soul for union with God in love. During this night, which is more painful than the earlier one, God secretly teaches the soul about the nature of true love, infusing contemplative knowledge of a more elevated kind than that which was learned during the night of sense.

Mystical writers call this infused contemplation a ray of darkness. As in the first night the wisdom is too much for the soul's capacity, and is consequently perceived as darkness. 'When the rays of this pure light strike upon the soul' says St John of the Cross, 'the soul perceives itself to be so unclean and miserable that it seems as if God had set Himself against it, and itself were set against God.' The prevailing temptation is now to think that all has been delusion, and that there is no return either to God or to creatures.

If bewilderment and anxiety were the pains particularly attached to the night of sense, the dominant suffering connected with the night of the spirit is loneliness. Abandoned, as it thinks, by God, the soul feels at the same time that human love is closed to it for ever.

Where before it was a case of worrying about not feeling, now the worry is about feeling too much. Where before it was the fear that nothing was being understood, now it is the fear that everything is being understood only too well.

Bereft of the three kinds of goods which the soul feels to be indispensable to its existence—namely natural, temporal, and spiritual—there is nothing to which the soul can look for support. It is like having the breath knocked out of you by a fall, and at the same time having your mouth covered so that you cannot re-fill your lungs with air.

The mystics tell us that the torments endured in this night of the spirit are comparable to those of hell, and that in any case they must amount to an anticipation of purgatory.

The particular kind of distress which this night engenders is not the kind which may be put down to natural melancholy. It does not see its life, as the melancholic sees his life, as a succession of unhappinesses. On the contrary, the soul in this condition of spiritual darkness, sees life as potential, but forbidden, happiness.

Memory serves only to remind the soul of the love which was at one time its habitual condition but which now is either irrecoverable or unwanted. To see itself alienated from charity, divine and human, is the deepest affliction to the soul.

The soul longs to forget but cannot forget, longs to find oblivion in death but cannot die, longs to be distracted if only for a little while from the pressing sense of loss and loneliness but cannot, even in the distractions which once delighted it, find the least relief.

If a spiritual director says that there is nothing to fear, he is not believed. Books are not the slightest use. The actual exercise of prayer is an agony. There is nothing to be done but to wait. It is the old night over again, but much worse.

But it must not be thought that the situation is black throughout. For one thing the two nights do not follow one another in quick succession: there is an interval between them during which the soul is being built up by grace and when the soul enjoys deep peace. For another thing there are periods during the second night when the soul sees clearly that all this suffering is meant, and that it is according to God.

It is while the soul is being treated to these interludes of reassurance that the understanding, which hitherto has had such a misleading influence, at last comes into its own. From having, as we have seen above, reported that it grasped the soul's condition and despaired of it, the understanding now brings consolation to the other faculties of the soul and admits that it has known nothing all along. The illuminative way is bearing fruit which the soul can appreciate.

St John of the Cross says that the night of the spirit may last, notwithstanding its vehemence, for some years. The length of it will depend upon how soon the soul can be rendered selfless enough to enter upon the unitive way, which is what the whole process has been leading up to.

Grace does not waste time, and when the powers of the soul are under the Holy Spirit's control—when they are entirely at the disposal of God, and as if their natural appetites did not exist—the soul begins to 'comprehend with all the saints what is the breadth and length and height and depth, and to know also the charity of Christ which surpasseth all knowledge'.

The soul, during those years of affliction in the two nights (but especially in the second), has been 'strengthened by the Spirit with might unto the inward man' so that Christ is now dwelling ever more fully by faith in the heart.

Surprised at its new-found conception of truth after so much fumbling and floundering, the soul walks on air for a while and is able without difficulty to acknowledge the cause of its development. It appropriates no merit; it gives the whole credit with gratitude to God.

The soul has been drawn away from its 'ordinary and common sense of things' and is now attuned to the divine and true sense. It cannot conceive how it ever failed to follow the workings of grace, nor how it manages to follow them now. It knows, without having to be told it, that the Spirit and not its own intellect 'searches all things, even the profundities of God.'

Commenting on this dawn which brings the second night to an end, St John of the Cross shows for once a lighter side. Everything that the soul hears and sees, he says, seems to it 'to be most strange and out of the way' because seen now in the light of truth, 'though in reality these things are, as they usually are, the same as what formerly occupied it'.

The soul is walking in the illuminative way—towards that which is called unitive.

THE HABIT OF PRAYER

SINCE it is a fact that in God we 'live and move and have our being', the act of recollecting ourselves is not one which makes demands upon our imagination so much as upon our attention. It is not a trick of the mind which makes us habitually prayerful, it is concurrence with the grace of God's habitual presence.

In order to pray outside the times of prayer as well as during them, the soul must get used to turning the successive events and changes of the day into vehicles of prayer. In this way the act of contemplation is expanded and extended into a contemplative attitude of mind.

When Dionysius told Timothy 'not to relax in the practice of mystical contemplation' he was not telling his disciple to be faithful in the specific exercise *only*; he was echoing St Paul's injunction to 'pray always and not to faint'. Just as the arrow goes on flying through the air after the bow has done its appropriate work, so contemplation goes on into the day after its act has been performed.

175

The bow-and-arrow simile serves well enough to illustrate the early stages of habitual prayer—the suggestion being that force is required before the arrow can leave the bow at all—but in the more developed stages of contemplation there is a gravitational pull which shifts the emphasis from propulsion to attraction.

The soul, habituated to contemplation, is drawn into itself—and so to the cause and centre of its desire, namely God—by the magnetism of a love which is not its own but God's.

Since God has expressed Himself more fully in human beings, made in His image, than in any other of His works, His activity will be felt as a compelling force according to the degree that the soul conforms to that image of Himself.

Where the attraction is one of affinity, the relationship must be closer and more constant than any other. The practice of the presence of God is based on the attraction of Himself to Himself in us.

Since God has given us a share in His life, since His being and His love are the reason for and substance of our being and our love, we should not find it too difficult to identify our activity with His. We can do this every time we unite ourselves with His will. And to do this habitually is to practise habitual prayer.

Acts that are done in virtue of God's love and in union with His will are as truly acts of prayer as is the worship that is given to Him in the liturgy or in contemplation. Passing naturally from the worship of God in choir to the worship of God in the cell or in the field, the soul transcends distinctions and forms, finding its real life in the presence of God.

Indeed not only does the soul rise above the natural which spells for it the supernatural, but, having risen, advances all the more surely for the help which the natural now provides.

Having discovered supernatural truth, we do not suddenly become different beings. What happens is that we become fully the beings that incompletely we are already. Contemplation, discovering to us the presence of God which has been present all along, is the grace which brings us from childhood to maturity. We are the same people underneath.

Living its life in the presence of Christ, the soul finds itself being true to its own nature for perhaps the first time in its experience. Indeed its own nature has been largely hidden from it until now. Fears and evasions have kept it out of sight.

Discovering its own identity, the soul appreciates at last the doctrine of identification. That God should, out of love, take the nature of man is wonderful enough, but that the Incarnation should be carried to lengths of identification with *this* man, myself, is beyond the power of gratitude to express.

For years the soul can be striving to attain to spiritual maturity and yet seem to get nowhere. Groping towards God, towards recollection, towards stability in His service, the soul learns nothing, apparently, from experience. Then, by the gift of grace, the whole scene changes and the years of effort are rewarded.

The new vision which is granted to the soul is felt to be so completely new as to bear no relation to the earlier and long-drawn-out peering through the mist. But in fact the connexion is very close: the scene and the horizon are the same; it is just the light on the hills that is different.

Under the secret guidance of grace, and in the dark nights, the soul has all along been unconsciously working towards precisely *this* illumination of precisely *this* sector of the landscape. The soul has all along been painfully handling outward as well as inward circumstances and secondary effects, marshalling them into what it forlornly hoped would somehow be counted for a supernatural pattern. And now, in the light of grace, the pattern is seen to have come out. It is a revelation.

Without his knowing it, every man is waiting for some such revelation. And when it comes it gives knowledge of God, of people, of the man himself. But almost always, like the revelation of Scripture, it is a revelation composed of human symbols; only here, instead of the symbols of words, the composition makes use of existing circumstances—the setting of the man's life. Again it is a case of the natural being expressed in God's supernatural terms.

If this is happening in the everyday life of the Christian who has no very clear call to interior prayer, what must be the silent under-the-surface preparation which habitual persevering prayer must effect in the soul whose whole purpose is God?

The acquisition of a virtuous habit, even allowing for the action of grace, is largely a matter of obstinately and consistently rejecting the evidence of failure. But it requires more than stubborn perseverance to establish a supernatural habit—whether of prayer or of anything else. It requires faith. The soul must have faith in the value of recollection as well as faith in the willingness of God to grant it.

The habit of recollection is up to a point dependent upon the soul's effort—the soul, acting under the impulse of grace, taking practical steps to live in the presence of God—and after that certain point dependent upon an infused gift of God. The infused gift in question is that of contemplation.

Thus it would be a mistake to think of habitual recollection as either exclusively the preparation for the set exercise of interior prayer or the necessary effect of the set exercise of prayer. It is both.

To show that habitual prayer is not an automatic consequence of graces received in prayer but a deliberate application of the mind, we have St John of the Cross saying of the soul which has advanced as far as the spiritual betrothals that 'it is now in its power to abandon itself whenever it wills to this sweet sleep of love'.

If the immediate preparation for the union of the soul with God is the surrender of self in the act of prayer, the remote preparation is the sustained surrender of self implied in the habit of looking always for God's will.

Though apparently distracted, and certainly often interrupted, the soul that wants only God's will is 'whether present or absent, always with the Lord'.

178

At every moment, by our desire to respond, we are straining towards Him who in any case 'is not far from every one of us'. In the Epistle to the Romans we read that 'the expectation of the creature is waiting for the revelation of the sons of God': the waiting is the work of recollection, is the life of faith.

'We know that every creature groaneth and travaileth in pain even till now. And not only it but ourselves also, who have the first-fruits of the Spirit, even we ourselves groan within ourselves, waiting for the adoption of the sons of God.' This, if we want to know what is meant by habitual prayer, is the text for us to study.

THE DEVELOPMENT OF PRAYER

IF Christ's spirit is to be developed in us, and not merely exhibited before us, the process by which we assimilate that spirit will have to be ever increasing in momentum and penetrating in depth. Since Christ whom we are seeking within ourselves is living and infinite, our search—if it is to be a reality and not a routine—must be living and progressive.

We do not copy a dead man; we co-live the life of a living Man. *Christi sumus, non nostri.* Our spirituality does not develop for the sake of our spiritual development; it develops in Christ for the sake of Christ.

If Christ is the alpha and omega, the beginning and end of all we do, He must be also the means by which we do it. He is the Way, and without Him we can do nothing. He is the Vine, and without the living sap we are dead branches.

When we talk about progress in the spiritual life, about the development of a soul in prayer, we are talking about Christ or we are talking about nothing. Christ is the only principle of progress. Prayer can never be the principle of its own progress. Nothing created can at the same time be its own *terminus a quo* and *ad quem*.

For the development of our prayer we rely upon the Spirit of Truth which will teach us all things. That Holy Spirit, which is the Spirit of the Father and of His Son, imparts to us the secret of advancement towards Himself. It is called sanctifying grace.

Because the part played in the soul's progress is more God's than man's, the progress is seen less by man than by God.

The more strictly interior the soul's life, the less apparent the depths, the stages, the progress.

Indeed it may be said that in the contemplative way of prayer, whatever there is of progress is seen in reverse and as failure.

In the natural order the realization of a new state, or the acquisition of a new knowledge, is accompanied by a sense of loss. It is a case of the frog having to sacrifice the happiness of the tadpole in order to enjoy the fuller happiness of the frog.

If a puppet were made into a man the first thought which would come into his head would be: 'But I cannot be a puppet any more … I am more at home with puppets than with men.' Growth hurts; change hurts.

Growth and change are not only painful but misleading. As the soul mounts towards the light of God, rising up out of the natural to meet the supernatural, there is a sense of loss. The soul feels that it is going backwards, downwards.

Souls far advanced in the spiritual life look back longingly at the fervours of their early years in prayer. Lacking such devotion now, they judge themselves to be less generous with God.

An aviator cannot, with the unaided eye, measure the height to which his plane has mounted since it took off from the ground. A fisherman sees the bed of a clear piece of water as almost touching the bottom of his boat. A contemplative soul, whose normal state is anyway one of darkness, can form no true idea of how far he has come in his search for God.

Spiritual development is not a matter of becoming more obviously perfect, but more perfectly Christlike.

Progress in prayer is not a matter of having a wider range or even a clearer vision; it is a matter of seeing in a different light and so with a different focus.

With each alternation between darkness and light the soul is being drawn along the way of prayer to God. There may be no understanding of the map, the milestones may be covered up, the signposts may be written in a foreign language. Nothing of this matters in the least. What matters is that the soul should 'grow unto the measure of the stature of the fullness of Christ'.

Growth towards the sufficiency of Christ is growth away from the insufficiency that is self. It is substituting a new life for the old. To live in Christ where before we lived in self is not merely to give a new direction to our effort, it is to receive a new vitality into our system. 'I live now, not I, but Christ.'

Having spent the whole of our spiritual life in thinking of Christ in a particular way it is bound to be confusing when we can think of Him so no longer, and must learn a new way. Mary Magdalen experienced this difficulty when she was told that she must know Him no longer according to a human mode of apprehension, and that she must wait for a more real and elevated knowledge.

So of course it is expedient for us that He should go, or the new revelation of Him will not come. So of course it is better that we should have faith and believe, than that we should have sight and imagine that we know all that there is to be known.

Mystical theologians tell us that this development in the spiritual life is not a change of knowing but a change of being, that the advance of the soul is not in degree only but in kind. God means to the soul all that He meant to it before, but not *as* He meant to it before.

They tell us that this alteration in its apprehension of God and of its own relationship with God is a radical alteration, involving structural adaptations as well as providing a new view. A new elevation rises on the old site. True spiritual growth, say the mystics, is not a getting bigger but a becoming other.

Be all this as it may, it makes souls who are thus advancing in the love of God doubt the way they have come, doubt their own good faith, doubt their ability to hold on for much longer. For them it is not to look back or to look forward—they will only make guesses if they do, and these will be wrong—but to trust in the immediate grace to carry them over the present. They must take it on faith that they are living a new life in a new element, and that God is seeing to their progress in a new dimension. And for none of this will the old standards of assessment serve.

How then can there be any assurance of being on the right way—let alone of advance Is the director's word the only indication—and how is even he to know?

The evidence, though valid enough, can but be indirect; it is proved by results. Souls cannot, while revealing the exterior and interior signs of fidelity, be going back on their surrender to grace. The signs may not be very clear to the soul, but to the soul's director they leave no doubt.

The outward effect of true advance in love is, on the authority of St Teresa, a deeper and less self-conscious detachment from creatures accompanied by a more realist application of the Passion. The soul thinks less about how to detach itself and more about how incompatible is love for the Passion and love for creatures.

The more inward effect is an increasing awareness of change in the relationship with God during the actual exercise of prayer. By no effort of the soul's part has this come about, and the soul knows it. Effort is the last thing the soul connects with what has passed for prayer. Experience points all the other way: there has not, according to the soul's estimate, been anything like enough effort.

Looking back, the soul can see that there was a time when the search for God took the form of exploring the various emotions which expressed the worship of God—praise, contritions, gratitude and so on—but now the search is both more orderly and more comprehensive.

The movement of the soul towards God has a unity and tranquillity not known hitherto. It flows like a deep river along an even course. In its action there are no sudden rushes of current; nor is it hampered by having to branch off into tributaries. While its progress is seen only from the bank— and not always very clearly from there—the waters from the land are moving forward to join the waters of the sea.

We have not come to test the speed of our progress towards God. It is not speed that counts but direction: if the soul is set towards God, wanting nothing but Him, that *is* progress.

THE TORMENT OF PRAYER

THE labour of prayer is more than the mere endurance of tedium or the effort to fight distraction. It can be, as the lives of contemplatives show, a positive pain. When the saints write about these things they have little difficulty in convincing us that the martyrdom of the spirit is more crucifying than the martyrdom of the flesh.

Nor in our enquiry do we have to go to the lives of the saints. We have material enough in Christ's 'Let this chalice pass from me' and 'My God, my God, why hast Thou forsaken me?' What was the purpose of Christ in disclosing these prayers to His Father if not to provide souls with them in their similar need?

What was the Holy Spirit's purpose in inspiring the psalmist to treat of the anguish which he experienced in his prayer if not to tell souls that they might be called upon to endure the same? To be consumed, to be brought low, to be left without relief, to be carried to the edge of despair: the expressions are there in the psalms, ready to be echoed by souls in their cries to God.

From devotional literature a man might gather that the whole of prayer was a warm, intimate, easy converse with God. He tries it, and perhaps at first his prayer confirms the impression. Only when he gives himself to the life of prayer does he find that it is a penance as well. And only when he gets on in the life of prayer does he find that it can be a torture.

If we make a list of what we expect to get from loving God, we shall find that it is the same as what we expect to get from loving people: the feeling of being understood, a sense of companionship and security, the knowledge that our affairs are capable of evoking pleasure or concern. We can rely, in a word, upon getting a response. The agony of prayer is precisely that we cannot rely upon this.

The soul can get no response whatever, and is consequently left to its own resources which experience has by now shown to be the merest shadow. Feeling itself to be unloving and unloved, the soul comes to dread the very exercise which has hitherto brought it its greatest peace. What is the good of doing something which only underlines one's loneliness, searches into one's empty spirit, reverses one's securities so that instead of confidence there is panic?

Where before the soul found expression in its prayer by ringing the changes from petition to gratitude, from penitence to praise, now, in a prayer which God has secretly unified, the soul can feel only one of two things: either that it is expressing itself or that it is not. And exactly half the agony of prayer is that it feels it is not.

The other half, caused by the feeling that God is not any longer communicating Himself to the soul, is equally a misconception. But misconceptions can deprive the mind of peace, of the sense of proportion, of hope.

It would be difficult to say whether the labour of this kind of prayer puts faith, hope, or love to the greatest strain.

Even outside prayer time, and with occupations to hold its interest, the soul is conscious of an abiding ache. During the time of prayer, the soul is ready to welcome with relief any interruption which is not of its own choosing. The idea of deliberately escaping is not entertained for a moment.

At an earlier stage the soul would have had to do violence to itself to meet the demand of a sudden interruption. Now it finds itself following the summons of charity with a light heart. This need not mean that the soul is habitually looking for an excuse to fly from the burden of its prayer; more probably it means that the recollection has gone deeper, and that there is nothing on the surface to show that it exists. You do not feel you are breaking a recollection which you do not feel to be there.

The burden of this prayer is described by St John of the Cross in his *The Spiritual Canticle*:

> Where hast Thou hidden Thyself,
> And abandoned me in my groaning, O my beloved?
> Thou hast fled like the hart,
> Having wounded me.
> I ran after Thee, crying;
> But Thou wert gone.

That the soul is in fact deeply recollected at a level which does not register superficial disturbance is further shown by the saint where, amplifying the above verse, he says that 'the Word, the Son of God, together with the Father and the Holy Ghost, is hidden in essence and in presence in the inmost being of the soul.'

In addition to the sense of loss which is the main suffering during this period, there is often an unexpected rebellion of the affections. To feel oneself thrown about by emotions which one had thought were dead and finished with is felt to give final proof that the whole course of prayer has been delusion from start to finish.

Again it is especially during the times of prayer that the trial is more particularly to the fore. While the depths of the soul is occupied with God, the surface is left free to observe with alarm the claims which these natural attractions make upon the sensitive appetite.

All the old issues which were thought to have been decided in the night of sense are revived; the human heart is seen to be active still. The humiliation is sharper now than was the

corresponding humiliation years ago. But the potential pleasure is felt to be just as keen.

Though they represent a danger—the affections always do—
these revived emotions are not likely to develop into anything
very serious. For one thing the significant activity of the will is
firmly in the Godward direction, and there is not a great deal
of energy to spare. It is not as in the crises of the past—when
the will was less fixed and the affection less broken by experience.

It is a mistake to think of the affections at any stage in the
spiritual life as ghosts only, as being merely a nuisance to
prayer. 'The soul must go out from all things in will and
affection ... and all things must be to it as if they existed not.'
These words of St John of the Cross are not, as might be
thought, taken from a passage describing the renunciations
required in the earlier purgative way; they come in the commentary between the stanza quoted above and the following:

> O shepherds, you who go
> Through the sheepcots up the hill,
> If you shall see Him
> Whom I love the most,
> Tell Him I languish, suffer, and die.

The affections, if they are taken to be a likely menace even
in the context here depicted, are not the elementary and harmless distraction which an over-indulgent director may sometimes take them to be.

It must not be supposed that the stage during which the
prayer of turmoil is experienced will last indefinitely. Prolonged beyond a certain point it would either affect the nerves
or else fail to act fruitfully upon the soul. So sooner or later the
tumult dies down, and the usual blankness takes its place.

But there is this difference between the state described and
other states, that it leaves behind a burnt-in sense of utter
nothingness.

This is not just exhaustion; it is the effect which grace has brought about by means of showing the soul how truly dependent it is upon God from crisis to crisis, from prayer to prayer, from temptation to temptation.

The soul, now fully convinced that it has failed God but been rescued by God, that it has gone out of its way to find satisfaction in creatures but has been failed by creatures, is more than ever disposed to throw itself, for what it is worth, into the arms of God.

As the result of its scorching and blinding prayer, the soul knows experimentally the truth that God is a consuming fire.

The Crowning of Prayer

FROM what has been said it will be noted that the life of prayer is subject to variations. Variations of temperature rather than variations of climate. While the prayer itself alters unaccountably—unaccountably anyway to the soul—the stages of prayer are found to follow a sequence.

That the sequence is intended in the Providence of God to lead to the highest knowledge and truest wisdom of which the soul is capable in this life is shown by St John's words from the *Ascent*: 'The soul will then dwell in this pure and simple light, transformed thereto in the state of perfection ... transformed in the pure and sincere Divine Wisdom who is the Son of God'.

Transforming union is the goal to which all the soul's fluctuating experience in the spiritual life has been tending. When the goal is reached the vicissitudes cease, and the tortuous way of perfection is made straight. The hills are levelled, the valleys are filled, and the brightness of Truth lights up the emptied soul with a love that is stable and at rest.

Because the soul is now so united within itself, and so caught up into the union of its whole being with God, there is no longer any worry about how the faculties of the soul are behaving. There is no awareness of disturbance—or indeed of self. The soul is made selfless in the fulfilment of love.

'The loving contemplative in the ground where he now rests' says Ruysbroeck describing this final stage, 'sees and feels nothing but an incomprehensible Light; and through that simple nudity which enfolds all things, he finds himself and feels himself to be that same Light by which he sees, and nothing else.'

Though such is the goal of the contemplative life, few souls of prayer are found to be of the purity which would let them attain to it. Somewhere along the way they are either afraid to go on or else satisfied with having got as far as they have. There are quantities of souls in the illuminative way, but very few in the unitive.

While still in the illuminative way, the soul may be given to enjoy unions with God in prayer during which it is conscious of 'the awful power of God beyond all other power and might, tastes of the wonderful sweetness and delight of the Spirit, finds its true rest and divine light, drinks deeply of the wisdom of God', but there is not yet the stability which is the mark of the unitive way.

Since the distinction is important—with an importance which is more than academic—a further passage from St John of the Cross must be quoted.

'In the state of betrothal, wherein the soul enjoys tranquillity and wherein it receives all that it can receive in this life, we are not to suppose its tranquillity to be perfect, but that the higher part of it is tranquil; for the sensual part, *except in the state of spiritual marriage*, never loses all its imperfect habits, and its powers are never wholly subdued as I shall show hereafter. What the soul now receives is all that the soul can receive in the state of betrothal, for in that of the marriage the blessings are greater.'

What the saint has hereafter to show may be summed up in his statement, confirming what we have already pointed out, to the effect that 'though the bride-soul has great joy in these visits of the Beloved in the state of betrothal, still it has to suffer from its absence, to endure trouble and affliction in the lower part and at the hands of the devil. *But all this ceases in the state of spiritual marriage.*'

The illuminative way, then, carries the soul to the climax of the betrothals, and the unitive way to the nuptials. But whereas the betrothals may be granted at any stage in the latter part of the illuminative way, the nuptials mark the beginning of the unitive way: union is the initiation.

The transformation of the soul is not effected in a single grace however unitive. The soul begins its transformation in the prayer of transforming union, and completes it in the habit of transforming union.

Though the important work, from the beginning of the spiritual course to the crowning climax, is not what the soul does for God but what God does for the soul, the serious intention of the soul throughout is the condition without which there is no reason to believe that God will do anything towards establishing the soul in the grace of contemplation. It is because souls lack this seriousness that their spirituality becomes a mere culture and not a life.

The man who is content to stand by and watch with loving admiration what he believes to be the manoeuvres of grace within his soul will get nowhere in the spiritual life. He has begun in a state of illusion, and is laying himself open to more dangerous deception later on. God does not choose to perform His work for souls unaided by souls.

There is all the difference between lying supine in the hands of God and surrendering one's activity to the activity of God.

The soul's purpose in prayer, as in everything else, is so to act that what is done may be done by God. The act is free, and is the soul's: the crowning of the act is also free, and is God's.

Even the repose of soul which comes with the consummation of prayer in the mystic marriage is not entirely passive, is not inertia or impotence. Ruysbroeck describes it as 'a loving self-emergence joined to a simple gazing into the incomprehensible Light'.

The consummation of prayer cannot be anything other than the consummation of perfection in Christ, and in Him the activity of perfection—even human perfection—cannot cease.

The crowning of prayer therefore—whether prayer be seen as an act, as an effort, as a life, as a grace, as a state—is the incorporation of the soul into the fullness of Christ.

Entitled by the sacrament of baptism to aspire to this union, the soul proceeds confidently, as a child by free adoption, through the trials and stages of the prayer life till it stands on the threshold of the Father's house. It is for the Father then, and when He wills, to come out with the crown in His hand.

While the soul is waiting, it can sing in the words of *The Spiritual Canticle*:

> My soul is occupied,
> And all my substance is in His service;
> Now I guard no flock,
> Nor have I any other employment:
> My sole occupation is love.

The soul knows by now that what the Father crowns is not the soul itself, nor its prayer nor its perfection; what the Father crowns is His Son whom He sees in the soul.

The union ratified in the Father's will, the soul, changing from the singular to the plural in its hymn of praise, later on invites the Beloved thus:

> Let us go forth to see ourselves in Thy beauty ...
> There we shall enter in
> And taste of the new wine of the pomegranate.
> There Thou wilt show me
> That which my soul desired;
> And there Thou wilt give me at once,
> O Thou, my life,
> That which Thou gavest me the other day.

If God is pleased with love above every other quality that man can express, here He finds it at its fullest human strength.

And because this human strength has power to please only in the measure that derives from, and partakes of, the love that is in Christ, its value is lifted from the human to the divine. It is so made wholly acceptable to the Father.

It is to this coronation, to this consummation, that the soul of prayer is incessantly tending. It is in its power to stop short at meditation, at forced acts, at the prayer of simple regard, or at any other stage of the spiritual way. But if it goes on, and if the grace is there, it is crowned.

How can God but crown what He Himself makes *coronabile?*

POWER MADE PERFECT

ACCORDING to human wisdom the plenitude of power is arrived at by adding power to power. According to St Paul power is made perfect in infirmity.

According to human wisdom the clever people have the right to lead and correct and generally manage the ignorant and improvident. According to St Paul the foolish has God chosen to confound the wise.

According to human wisdom the quality above all to be disguised so that it appears as something else is weakness. According to St Paul it is weakness that compels the assistance of grace.

In its journey towards God in prayer the soul's whole guarantee of security rests on its confessed incapacity, weakness, nothingness. Convinced of its inability to meet the implications of the call, the soul is safe. 'When I am weak, then am I strong.' Otherwise not.

More, if the power of Christ is to dwell in me—and it must or I shall be without hope in this life—I shall have to learn to glory in my infirmity and in the cross of Christ. My insufficiency is my hope, not my shame. The thought of it is not something to be stifled, fled from. It is the means by which I enter into the wounds of Christ.

What else can St Paul mean when he says that our

sufficiency is from God, and that we have a 'confidence through Christ in God' but 'not as if we are sufficient to think anything of ourselves as of ourselves'?

Having told us that 'no flesh should glory in God's sight' St Paul makes a single exception—namely the glory that the human man is prepared to experience in the cross of Christ—and when we examine this exception we see that it is not the flesh that glories but the spirit. It is the spirit that glories in Christ's triumph over the flesh.

When the soul has passed in review the course of asceticism and spirituality that lies open to it, the thought at the back of the mind must be that of St Paul in his warning to the Corinthians: 'other foundation no man can lay but that which is laid, which is Christ'.

Though it might be objected that these texts from St Paul confirm only what is already known by anyone familiar with Christian thought, the truth contained is practical as well as theoretical. The knowledge that the success of human effort rests solely on grace should lead to the habit of seeing the failure of human effort equally in the scheme of grace.

Where the life of Christ is understood to touch the soul's life not only as an influence from without but as the life of the soul itself—real life with its trials and failures—the texts about glorying in the cross of Christ are fulfilled in fact.

Souls who have set out with the purpose of loving and serving God alone will come sooner or later to the conviction of having completely failed. The degree of their original expectation will be the degree of their disappointment. If their hope has been human, their disillusion will be complete.

But if the hope of the soul has been trust in God and not trust in the soul's power to reach God, there will be neither despair nor bitterness. There will be the same hope that there was all along, but now made purer because tried.

It is not that pessimism is turned as if by magic into optimism. It is that the soul has seen the worst, and has taken it to mean the best. This is not the effect of a trick; it is the effect of faith.

Nor is it that the soul, having abandoned all hope of finding true peace, has persuaded itself that peace of a sort may be found in having abandoned it.

It would be more true to say that the soul, having seen how insubstantial all things are in themselves, has learned to look for an explanation of them in their revelation of God.

The soul that is truly wise argues from the shadow to the substance, and then back again to the shadow. The shadow is now seen in its own right—as a shadow. But even shadows have their importance, and this is the first thing the soul sees when it realizes what they are the shadows of.

That personal failure reflects the failure and frustration of the Passion, that earthly peace reflects the peace which Christ alone can give, that loneliness and pain reflect the Agony — these appreciations of supernatural truth give to the soul a security and a perspective and a grasp on life which it is beyond the power of earthly wisdom to provide.

It is not psychology but faith that tells us to 'look not at the things that are seen but at the things that are not seen, for the things that are seen are temporal but the things that are not seen are eternal.'

When the things that are seen are rightly seen, they point not to the temporal but to the eternal. 'The invisible things of God are clearly known, being understood by the things that are made.' But we need a revelation to tell us this.

Human infirmity then, seen in this way as a reflexion, does make power perfect; the folly of the cross does outshine the wisdom of the wise; the poor in spirit do possess the greatest wealth; those who are the most like little children are in fact the really great.

So of course there is no morbid stress or oratorical exaggeration in the claim of St Paul to glory in the cross of Christ. It is the entirely sensible thing for a man of faith to do.

We do not have to wait until we attain to the beatific vision before enjoying a share in the power of God. 'The Lord is my strength'—already.

'If any man thirst let him come to Me': if any man is weak

let him come to Christ. As thirst is the condition for the satisfaction of thirst, so weakness is the condition for the satisfaction of weakness.

True power dwells in emptiness not in plenitude. Even human power when at its noblest, as in moral justice, is marked more by its reserves than by its expressions of force. And what greater power has human history revealed than that which was shown by Christ when He emptied Himself becoming obedient unto death.

For us who are the weak things of the world, and the foolish, our strength lies in Him to whom all power is given in heaven and on earth. Therefore can we safely glory in our infirmities, and in nothing else save in His Passion which they reflect.

FAITH MADE PERFECT

JUST as 'I can do all things in Him who strengthens me', so I can believe all things in Him who is the object of my belief.

Dominus illuminatio mea et salus mea.[1] I am not my own light nor my own salvation. My faith goes to Him because it comes from Him. My salvation is His.

'What do you ask of the Church of God?' is the question addressed to the soul before baptism. 'Faith' is the answer. When the soul is incorporated into Christ at baptism, it enters the world of faith.

Beginning in baptism, faith goes on through the soul's life expanding every opportunity and enriching every experience with an increasing inflowing of light.

But light, as we have seen, may often appear as darkness to the soul of faith. So just as power is made perfect in infirmity, faith is made perfect in the darkness of doubt.

What the soul has above all to remember before, during, and after the trials of its faith is that its search after God in obscurity is really the search on the part of God after itself.

[1] 'The Lord is my light and my salvation.'

If the soul allows God to search in vain, the result is unhappiness in this life and in the next. Such is the frightening liberty of man's will. But if God is allowed to take up the soul into Himself, with the full implications of baptism realized, there is happiness for the soul now and for ever.

If we let God into the soul, into every cell of it, He goes surety for the reality of our faith. Not only for the conviction of faith, but for the perfection of faith.

For God to take the soul into His confidence, there must be complete confidence on the part of the soul. 'If we desire to experience eternal life in our own selves' says Ruysbroeck, 'we must, passing beyond reason, first enter into God by faith. There we must remain, simple, despoiled of all images and lifted by love into an open nakedness in our higher memory.'

It is because we trust in other securities besides God that we are left to other securities. For the perfection of faith there must be no other securities whatever. If to trust in creatures is folly—as for example in money, in health, in human love, in either the settled arrangement of circumstances or the possible change of circumstances—it is no less folly to trust in knowledge, strength of character, spiritual experience.

If we stop short at anything less than God Himself, our trust is incomplete. It is not enough for us to believe because of what our belief will bring us: for faith made perfect we must believe because of God.

Instinct takes us some of the way; reason takes us some of the way; it is grace alone that takes us the whole way.

Grace acts through instinct; grace acts through reason; it is through divine love that grace finds its most appropriate channel.

Natural instinct, unaided by grace, is not a virtue; nor is the purely natural understanding virtuous. 'Faith has no merit' says St Gregory, 'where human reason supplies the proof.' It is the life of faith, and only the life of faith, that gives merit in the sight of God.

The knowledge which comes to the soul of pure faith is

two-fold: in one direction it relates to God, in the other to creatures. In each direction the knowledge deepens in the measure
that the soul corresponds with the grace of contemplative
prayer.

In regard to God the soul finds itself entering, without
direct application of the mind, into the meaning of God's
attributes. God's goodness, omnipresence, providence, mercy
—every divine perfection—can now be understood as realities
where before they were seen only as theoretical applications.

Hitherto, and when the occasion served, the soul has dwelt
upon the attributes separately. Now the soul seems to live in
the atmosphere of the divine attributes, hardly distinguishing
between their several functions but seeing them as facets of the
same stone, as windows of the same lamp.

The soul knows that none of this can be accounted for
otherwise than in the most general terms, and that it bears
little or no relation to the knowledge acquired from books. All
the soul knows now is that, whatever the explanation of it, the
knowledge brings an exquisite peace and happiness. The
delight experienced in these flights of the purified intellect outweighs past suffering. Indeed for a time it seems to block out
the trials of the spirit altogether from the memory; certainly
it makes present tribulations feel light.

In regard to creatures, the soul, enjoying its new apprehension of faith, has entered upon a new relationship with the
external world. In a sense it has come to terms with the world.
As uncompromising as ever towards worldliness, the soul is
able at last to see the world with the eyes of faith. What this
really means is that the soul has come to terms with the
Incarnation.

Not until the soul is free of creatures can it truly delight in
creatures. Not until creatures have been hidden behind the
cloud of forgetting may they come out into the light of remembering. It is only now that the memory is cleared of images.

But once the memory, together with the other faculties of
the soul, is fully united to God in the perfect life of faith, the
knowledge of creatures is made true. No longer is the vision of

creatures coloured by concupiscence. The desire for them is unspoiled by possessiveness; it has only their own good and God's in mind.

It is not so much that faith controls desire as that it unites it with the desire that is in Christ. 'With desire have I desired to eat this pasch with you.' By faith we come to share a love in which there is no self.

Where at an earlier stage the soul, bereft of every creaturely satisfaction could sing—in the words of St John of the Cross's poem—

> Forth unobserved I went,
> My house being now at rest.
> In darkness and in safety,
> By the secret ladder, disguised,

it can now, purified by the nights, and in far greater safety, use creatures without harm. The soul has discovered truth at last—truth about God and about the delights with which He has surrounded us. The song now is

> The bride has entered
> The pleasant and desirable garden,
> And there reposes to her heart's content;
> Her neck reclining
> On the sweet arms of the Beloved ...
> Our bed is of flowers ...
> Hung with purple,
> Made in peace,
> And crowned with a thousand sheets of gold.

Thus is the soul defended and built up in faith. Now the activity of love can be exercised without the distraction of having to sort out and direct and sanctify. All this, which was once such a worrying process, is done for the soul by God.

'Being now free from all molestation of natural affections, and a stranger to the anxiety of temporal affairs, the soul enjoys in security and peace the participation of God.' St John does not tone down the language which he uses when treating of the life of faith. The contemplative soul, praying in faith, 'partakes,' he says, 'of the perfections of God.'

No wonder, then, that the catechumen's answer to the Church's question at baptism 'What dost thou ask of the Church of God?' is simply 'Faith'. It is faith that begins the life of hope and love, and in this life completes it. Though love is the fulfilling of the law, it is faith that shows love how to fulfil the law. Without faith it is impossible to love.

Hope Made Perfect

THE life of man on earth is like a lamp waiting to be lit, a bowl waiting to be filled, a violin waiting to be played. Hope is the quality which keeps man waiting in faith. Hope is made perfect when the soul waits its consummation not only in faith but in love.

But for hope to prove itself in love it must wait on and on in faith and patience. Through doubt, discouragement, near despair, a sense of the utter hopelessness of everything, the soul perfects its hope. Hope is made perfect, then, not in fulfilment but in frustration.

The trial of hope, which is the work of grace, is effected both by interior desolations and exterior circumstances. Regarding the former, the course to be pursued is one of unquestioning perseverance. Regarding the latter, unconditioned flexibility.

It is often the case that God makes use of man's mistakes to bring about the perfection of a virtue. Hope, in its purest form, is elicited from the soul as the result of corrections which have had to be administered to false modes of perception, to errors of spiritual and practical judgment, to natural immaturities.

The mistake above all which leads to the blocking of hope, natural and supernatural, is that of allowing a security or a perfection to be built up in the mind to the exclusion of the security and perfection desired by God. The only corrective to such a misconception, which is fashioned by imagination and desire, is frustration—frustration precisely of imagination and desire.

What is the complaint made by those who are in the dark night of hope? Is it not 'this is quite different from what I was led to expect; it is not what I bargained for; it bears no relation to the highest cravings of my soul ... and therefore I have despaired of finding happiness'?

But one does not *expect*—one gives. One does not bargain with love. One's soul may crave, but let the craving be for God and His will, and not for what one thinks God and His will must be like.

To crave a preconceived perfection must inevitably lead to disappointment. The whole idea is that there is no preconceived perfection, no anticipated security, no applied achievement. The design into which the soul must fit can be seen by God alone. For the soul to be able to see it, and to see itself fitting into it, would be to spoil not only the purpose but the pattern. It would become a pretty composition, not a perfect one.

Also the soul follows the law of growth: its conceptions change with maturity. Perfection, happiness, suffering—these things have a different meaning for the neophyte and for the saint.

The happiness of the child may be either more or less untroubled than that of the man, but the point is that it is not at all the same as the man's. The child expects life to go on as it is going on now, providing the satisfactions that it knows; the man, having learned from experience, sees happiness as something which has to be earned, which has to be safeguarded, which is not by any means a common commodity.

The child does not reason about happiness, or look for it in one place rather than in another; the man knows that if there is to be any security at all, he must place his desire beyond the reach of human disappointment: his treasure must be proof against rust, moth, thief.

The child looks forward to *more* life; the man, if he is wise, looks forward to another life. The child has only physical experience to go by; the man knows that physical experience is not enough.

The child, if not taking it entirely for granted, views the future as an increasingly adventurous present. The man sees the future as the result of many contributive causes. Adventure, for the man, hardly enters in. For him it is a question of balanced choices—and if he is a man of faith it is a question of grace.

Happiness for the man is a serious business: no coloured dreams, no guesswork, no idle wishing. Like the child he must be expectant, but where the child is vaguely and naturally hopeful the man must practise deliberate and supernatural hope.

But fortunately God treats us all as children: while our eyes see next to nothing of the true meaning of life, our feet are placed by Him in the right way of truth. We make mistakes, we think we have come to the end of our strength, we say we have given up hope, and all the while He has been drawing us along towards Himself. 'Strange-visaged blunders, mystic cruelties ... I know Him for I love Him.'

Hope, like faith, is made perfect in its contradictions, inconsistencies, anomalies. How else can its essential antitheses be overcome? Presumption can be denied only by denying the implications of humanism; despair by the depending upon God alone.

Nor is it when worldly securities are removed that the soul is most tried in hope, most left alone to depend upon God. It is when the spiritual supports are taken away, and the soul feels helpless and weak, that hope is tested in perfection.

But unless his spiritual ambitions are denied, how can a man's self-hood be properly abased? For the necessary transformation in grace a man must be annihilated in his own eyes—and sometimes in the eyes of others.

The final test comes when the ideal which looked so clear, and which possessed such a compelling attraction when we first started painting it on the walls of our minds years ago, no longer means a thing.

When the Magi drew close to Bethlehem, the star went out. We ask for information, and we get different answers. There is no light, and we are in a foreign land. This is where the secret hope which we have been storing up for years comes to our rescue and tells us what to do next. Not that we suddenly see a way out, or that at the moment of breaking we feel a renewal of hope welling up inside us, but that without our being able to trace the process of the change we find ourselves going on.

Hope requires of us that we not only go on and on, but that we go on with Christ, which means without bitterness and in love. Our experience is meant to have drained our natures of self-pity, self-dramatization, and the sourness which comes of rebellion against God's handling of our lives. We have put on a new personality. By hoping only in the Person of Christ we are ourselves no longer.

The only sadness now is the knowledge that souls are missing this source of happiness, this hope. Why must so many flounder about in their despair when the solution to the agonized questing of their souls is attainable in Christ? Thus the soul of hope, kept sane now no longer solely by the thought that a satisfaction must exist to its longing if only the formula can be discovered, is on fire to point out to others the grounds of its new-found confidence.

When the foundations of life are seen to be grace, when the whole sustaining power of one's vocation is understood as the life of Christ, hope is as instinctive an expression of one's prayer as faith. Hope and faith breathe out prayer as prayer breathes out hope and faith. Which is love.

Just as hope could not be made perfect without prayer, so prayer could not be made perfect without hope. And neither could be made perfect without love.

That the object of hope must be out of reach in this life is the condition of hope; that the object is pre-viewed by faith is the proper activity of hope; that the deferring of hope's fulfilment is endured in love is hope's perfection.

201

'THE highest testimony of love that a soul can give' says
St Thomas, 'is to set aside all that belongs to this present
life, and to find its happiness in giving itself up exclusively to
the contemplation of God.' That contemplation should be the
supreme witness to love would be denied by many who place
their trust in active works. But those who have passed from
activity to contemplation know it to be true.

'Is it not an even higher testimony' the active soul will ask,
'to lay down one's life for God?' Martyrdom is indeed a consummation of love, but what St Thomas is thinking about here
is not the martyrdom of the body but the martyrdom of the
spirit. The mystic vocation may not be crowned as martyrdom
is crowned, but it is a laying down of life for God nevertheless.
The shedding of blood is the moment of climax; contemplative
perfection is the work of a lifetime.

In any case, whatever we happen to think about it, the
authorities are agreed that there is no greater glory that man
may give to God than the worship which he may give in the
mystic vocation. 'One act of pure love' says St John of the
Cross, 'is worth more to God, to the Church, and to the soul,
than any quantity of active works of zeal.'

Souls pledged in this way to an interior service, though unconscious of light and registering little of truth, reflect the
light and bear witness to the truth. To them there is no longer
resistance to grace. They are enlarged by grace, and they communicate it to others. And in this way they fulfil the twofold
office of charity.

In the perfection of charity there is an increase, not a
decrease, in the service given to others. St Thomas says of such
service that it is not something subtracted from contemplation
but something which, though it springs from it, is comple-
mentary to contemplation—is added to it.

One reason why we never fully resolve the difficulty of serving what appear to be two masters in this matter of charity is
that we never really understand how Christ loves us.

The charity which we show to God is His love in us. The charity which we show to others and which they show to us is His. Once we understand that the love which attracts and absorbs our love—whether the object of our love is immediately God or our neighbour—is God's love made recognizable, we find ourselves drawn into unity instead of divided into separate loyalties.

Perfect charity imparts and receives charity without self. Souls who know that they are nothing do not think of attracting love to themselves. Nor do they claim any personal ability in imparting it. They are selfless. They know that there is nothing in themselves, as of themselves, to which love could be attracted. They know too that there is nothing in themselves, as of themselves, which is worth handing on to others. So they become unblocked channels of grace—grace moving both ways.

Were we not first the recipients of God's love, we could neither awaken love in others nor respond to it. Were we not made in God's image, and were others not made in the same image, there would be no point in awakening love in others or responding to it. The point of love is God, and everything else about it must minister to this.

The love of our neighbour is more clearly defined than almost any other doctrine in Scripture. The epistles and gospels are full of it. Though we know well enough that we must love our neighbour as ourselves, we are less clear about the duty of loving him as Christ loves us. But Christ's love is the key to the whole thing.

We must love not only *because* Christ loves, but *as* Christ loves. We must aim at loving in the same way that He does. It is not a parallel emotion; it must be an identical emotion. If this is to mean anything at all, it must mean that His whole life must be my whole life, and my whole life must be His. And if *this* is to mean anything at all, and not remain dead on the page as a literary flourish, it must mean that I must pray myself into His mind and heart, and think of nothing but loving Him alone.

Christ invites of us—indeed elicits from us if we once completely give in to Him—expressions of the precise emotion which was His ruling emotion during His life on earth. He wants us to give to one another, and to Him, the identical thing that He gave, and now gives, to us. He is satisfied with nothing short of the best that can be given, which is His love.

It is *His* love that we must give: there is no love, worthy of the name of love, that is not His. The love that He wants is the selfless love that comes from Him and must go back, still selfless, to Him.

The saints are those whose love is so completely de-selfed that the Spirit of God can speak through them, can shine through them. The saint is like flawless glass whose thickness is no obstacle to the light which penetrates it. Those who are not saints, those whose love is mixed with human loves, are like windows of stained glass: the light which they let in is coloured by their desires and broken up into patterns by the lead of their too-human temperaments. Those who are not trying to do the will of God are like blackened panes through which the light cannot come: the sun beats upon such windows, and the only result is that the darkness becomes airless as well.

The reason why God wants love from man is not that He lacks anything that man can give to Him but that, possessing the plenitude of love, He wants man to share its fullness with Him.

Christ stoops to the level of man that He may win the heart of man, which, if what it contains is truly love, is His own love made imitable.

St Gregory has been quoted on an earlier page as saying that 'faith has no merit where human reason supplies the proof'; so neither has charity any merit where human affection supplies the motive. Only when ordered towards God can human affection be material for the praise of God. Only when the human heart is raised in homage and obedience to the divine heart, can the love of one another be identified with the love of God. When this happens, then may St Augustine's 'Love God, and do what you will' be safely followed.

Once you love, you see the reason for what before was without reason. Love explains everything. It does not excuse everything but it explains everything. It explains the inexplicable.

Love alone gives its full importance to life, taking up into itself life's unimportances. It is love that makes men do the unimportant things as though they were important things— because of the importance of Christ who dwells within their souls and does these unimportant things through them. It is also love that makes men do the important things as though they were unimportant—because of the selflessness with which they are done.

Love in the same way gives its value to the observance of the law. The reason why love is the fulfilling of the law is that without love the law is pointless. If all authority comes from God, all obedience is designed to go back to God. Obedience, like prayer and works of outward charity, is an expression of love.

If you miss the point of obedience to the law, it is the same as if you missed the point of prayer or works of outward charity: you make a meritless burden of what is meant to be an act of love.

If you look upon the rules of religion as hurdles and not as helps, you have not begun to understand the law of love. If you look upon the rules of religion as a substitute for the law of love, you have not begun to understand religion. Religion is love and love is religion.

KNOWLEDGE MADE PERFECT

TO develop in love is to develop in the divine life, and to develop in the divine life is to develop in all things. Just as the whole organism of the Church continues to 'grow up in Him who is the head, even Christ, from whom the whole body, being compacted and fitly joined together, by what every joint supplieth, according to the operation in the measure of every part, maketh increase of the body unto the edifying of itself in charity', so in the individual soul there is a corresponding growth in Christ. All the time, allowing that the soul is placing no obstacles in the way, the process is going on. Grace is prompting the goodwill of the soul and the soul's goodwill is inviting further grace.

Man's only progress amounts to this—that he enters more and more fully into the perfection of Him who is the life and the light of men. This is the only true wisdom. There is no other way than Christ, no other truth, no other freedom. His is the only life by which a man may live without walking in darkness. His is the only light which exposes the errors and evils which are hidden in worldliness. It is a straight issue: Christ or this world. To see this is at least to make a start in wisdom; to act upon it, and live by it, is wisdom indeed.

What some people call knowledge others call experience. Whether you take it as the fruit of study, suffering, prayer—or a combination of the three—the resulting wisdom is the work of grace. That is why it is in ignorance, as much as in the acquisition of knowledge, that wisdom is made perfect. 'There is a more perfect knowledge of God' says Dionysius, 'which results from a sublime ignorance.'

This knowledge, of which the mystics speak as being the highest apprehension of God, is knowledge by love. It comes through what John of St Thomas calls 'union by the inviscera-tion of God in ourselves'. It is a knowledge which, to quote again from Dionysius, 'is brought about by virtue of an incomprehensible union and is the result of a sublime ignorance.' It is in the thick of the cloud of unknowing that the light of knowledge made perfect begins to shine.

The mystic ideal is not confined to the achievement of a specific perfection; rather it represents the closest possible assimilation and union with God. Boldly the mystics speak of it as 'deification'. But confining ourselves to the practical implications, we can say this about the mystical ideal—that it supposes a striving to be identified with the infinite sanctity of

God. Then, when we look at this mystical ideal, we see that it amounts to no more and no less than the ideal proposed to every baptized Christian. All should be aiming at configuration in all things with Christ. All should be handing themselves over to possess, and to be fully possessed by, the Holy Spirit.

'We shall be like unto Him, for we shall see Him as He is.' Until then, our wise course is to admit that we know nothing. What we see of Him we see only in darkness, and this knowledge we cannot communicate. We know more by not knowing than by speculating, more by forgetting than by remembering, more by loving than by imagining.

'Then what does the soul do in its prayer' will be the question, 'if it has nothing recognizable towards which it must grope?' This difficulty is answered by Tauler, where he says: 'It attaches itself to nothing whatever, but stays naked and isolated; for if it rested on anything, that thing would necessarily be some image. It takes, then, for its share the sufferings and the cross of love.' Back again at the naked longing of love, ineffable and unsatisfied.

'But how can this state be described as possessing knowledge?' the soul enquires, 'when it seems to be nothing but a succession of obscurities, desolations, misgivings, and aridities.' For answer it should be pointed out that the fruits of the Holy Ghost bear witness to the presence of His gifts, and that true wisdom and knowledge are revealed in the soul that consistently and heroically exercises the acts of the Spirit.

It is precisely in the state of obscurity, bitterness, doubt, loneliness, and so on that the authentic quality of perfected knowledge is brought out. Thus the gift of fortitude produces the fruit of patience, the gift of fear produces longanimity, faith, meekness and the rest.

The soul that is making every effort to express joy in its sufferings, to maintain peace in its disturbances, to yield lovingly to what appears to be the harshest treatment, is attaining to the highest degree of supernatural knowledge. It is learning directly, experimentally, and practically from Wisdom Itself.

Partaking thus in Christ's Passion, the soul is enjoying the gift of understanding: it is entering into the mysteries of God's will. The bitterness has purified its wisdom, the hurtful kind of fear has deepened the fear which is of the Spirit. The soul is hungering and thirsting after justice—with a hunger and thirst that are all the more real because past their first pangs and now unfelt.

'But is it?' you will say. '*Is* the will stretching out to what it does not know and feel? How can the maximum of desire be kept up on the minimum of recognizable knowledge? Is it not an axiom that *nihil volitum, quin praecognitum?*'[1] On the authority of St Francis de Sales we have it that love more readily lends itself to be felt in the will than intelligence in the understanding. And St John of the Cross, in his commentary on the third stanza of the *Dark Night*, gives as one of the characteristics of the night of the spirit that the soul travels with no other guide or light but the love which burns within it and which sends it mounting up to God.

As a practical measure, therefore, the soul should avoid making efforts to realize its knowledge. The knowledge is now infused, and, of necessity, vague. All that the soul has to do is to allow itself to be drawn along by the obscure attraction of love. A too close examination of motive would resist, just as the least conscious selfishness would resist, the development of grace in the soul. The instinctive movement towards Love Itself would be, if not checked, considerably slowed down.

Again the puzzled enquirer might reasonably feel that there was danger here of illuminism, and that to follow one's instinct without the guarantees provided by the intellect would be to leave the door wide open to error. St Thomas replies to this objection where he speaks of contemplative souls being moved 'by a true divine instinct'. God's inspirations are ordinarily received unconsciously, the soul feeling prompted by an urgent longing which it cannot account for. The indistinct sense of wanting to love is quite enough: no need to know how

[1] 'Nothing is willed that is not already known.'

it got there, what it is composed of, how it will express itself, or what exactly it is wanting to love.

The impulse to identify oneself for ever with the supreme good and the source of love is of its nature bound to escape analysis. It is nevertheless a truly good impulse, springing from grace and adding to supernatural knowledge. 'God can readily infuse love and increase it without infusing or increasing *distinct* knowledge,' says St John of the Cross. The same authority goes on to explain that 'this is the experience of many spiritual persons, who find themselves burning in the love of God without having a more distinct knowledge of Him than heretofore. They can understand little and love much—just as they can understand much and love little.'

Since the gifts of the Holy Ghost do not depend upon learning but upon grace, the impulses to which they give rise are impulses of inspiration rather than of reason. It is not always that the interior life of a soul is a conscious life; more often it is lived on a plane which does not admit of conscious perception at all. Its activity is therefore instinctive.

It is a mistake to think of instinct as being inferior to reasoned choice. Instincts may act with a sureness and strength superior to the sureness and strength which derive from an awareness of the divine dispensation to which they relate. In such cases it is quite enough that the divine dispensation is divine.

The process is easier to follow if we look at it from God's angle rather than from man's. God, requiring of the soul the expression of a certain virtue or the taking of a particular decision, infuses light and knowledge which are so secretly received that the soul knows nothing of what has happened. All that the soul knows is that it feels instinctively impelled to follow a certain course.

The soul may never know the real motives of its action, may even judge that it has acted according to nature, but under the cover of external circumstance the Spirit of God has elicited the required result. This gives one more reason for seeing in external circumstances the signified will of God.

But for the soul to be so moved by the spirit there has to be great detachment, complete disinterestedness. There would be danger, for example, of the soul sheltering behind this doctrine and yielding to every passing whim. It is easy to pretend that we have the Holy Spirit behind us when in fact we have a selfish purpose in front of us.

So deep-seated can be our self-deceptions that there is no safety but in surrender to the action of God. Admitting that our own knowledge is only likely to lead us astray we enter confidently into the cloud of ignorance.

In Solomon's prayer for wisdom we have the answer to the problem. 'Send her' the wise man asks, 'that I may know what is acceptable with Thee ... she shall lead me soberly in my works and shall preserve me by her power. So shall my works be acceptable. For who among men is he that can know the counsel of God? And who can think what the will of God is? For the thoughts of mortal men are fearful, and our counsels uncertain.' We know nothing, and the Spirit knows all ... why do we hesitate to enter blindly into His wisdom?

'For the corruptible body is a load upon the soul, and the earthly habitation presseth down the mind that museth upon many things.' Perhaps this is our great mistake—that we must be forever musing upon many things. If the earthly habitation did not weigh upon the mind we might muse with profit, but the body is still corruptible and the soul can never in this life be absolutely true to itself: there is always the bias of original sin.

'And hardly do we guess aright at things that are upon the earth; and with labour do we find the things that are before us.' It is bad enough to be faced with the uncertainties of material living, 'but the things that are in heaven who shall search out?'

But Solomon is no existentialist. If his humanism has proved a broken cistern, at least he does not despair of a solution to the problem of life. His gift of understanding, his virtue of hope, his faith in the power of grace—these qualities lead him to round off his prayer in the authentic mystical tradition:

'Who shall know Thy thought except Thou give wisdom,

and send Thy Holy Spirit from above? And so the ways of men on earth may be corrected, and souls may learn the things that please Thee. For by wisdom they were healed, whoever have pleased Thee from the beginning.' There is no other super-natural wisdom than this for man to learn: his knowledge is made perfect in dependence.